Stories Economists Tell

Stories Economists Tell

Studies in Christianity and Economics

JOHN P. TIEMSTRA

PICKWICK *Publications* · Eugene, Oregon

STORIES ECONOMISTS TELL
Studies in Christianity and Economics

Pickwick Publications
An Imprint of Wipf and Stock Publishers
199 W. 8th Ave., Suite 3
Eugene, OR 97401

www.wipfandstock.com

ISBN 13: 978-1-61097-680-0

Cataloguing-in-Publication Data

Tiemstra, John P.

    Stories economists tell : studies in Christianity and economics / John P. Tiemstra.

    xiv + 192 pp. ; 23 cm. Includes bibliographical references.

    ISBN 13: 978-1-61097-680

    1. Economics—Moral and ethical aspects. 2. Economics—Religious aspects—Christianity. I. Title.

HB72 .T60 2012

Manufactured in the U.S.A.

Contents

Contents

Preface

I HAVE LONG BELIEVED that a conscientious effort to integrate the truth of Christianity with the practice of economics requires that the economist think of persons as moral agents rather than as narrowly self-interested calculating machines. This perspective requires dropping the customary assumptions of received economic thought in favor of a thoroughly different understanding of the nature of the person and the foundations of human behavior. This is a daunting task for anyone socialized in the modern economics profession.

Most of us who try to make this transition begin with a study of economic methodology (in the philosophy-of-science sense). What parts of received economics can we keep, and what do we have to replace? What sides should we take in the many scientific disputes in the economics profession? What is the relationship between economic analysis and policy prescription? What should we teach our students? We have to reach at least provisional answers to these questions in order to make any progress at all. There is a substantial literature addressing these issues, and the first section of this book contains my major work in this area.

However, we can easily get stuck in these methodological prolegomena, and never move on to the actual analysis. This is dangerous for several reasons. One has to do with credibility within the profession. If we always do philosophy of economics, but never economic analysis, is it even possible to do analysis of the sort we are looking for? If we complicate economics in an effort to make it more realistic and more morally relevant, do we remove the possibility of ever reaching conclusions? It's hard enough to reach definitive conclusions in economics, as all the old jokes suggest.

A Christian approach to economics needs to be morally relevant, because Christians will draw economic conclusions and make policy recommendations, sometimes even in the name of the church, whether we economists can provide a solid analytical foundation for them or not. The current debates within the church about globalization, climate change, poverty, and unemployment are only the most recent examples. Should the church not have economic analysis that is informed by Christian moral reflection?

If we wish to influence the broader profession, we must recognize that most economists have a strong pragmatic streak. Most of us are well-meaning introverts who want to improve society and help people (though without actually having to, you know, talk to them). An economics that is stuck at the methodological level does not scratch the economists' pragmatic itch.

The remaining three sections of the book chronicle my attempts to provide an economic analysis that takes persons seriously as moral agents, and pursues the implications of trying to apply Christian moral principles to economic life. Most of this involves ways of finding space in a market economy to make moral choices. I draw on some of the tools of conventional economic thought, particularly the analysis of imperfectly competitive markets and government regulation. I also access some of the riches of the social economics tradition, which began more than a century ago in Europe as a way to work out some implications of the newly developing Catholic social doctrines in the context of an industrializing society.

The second section of the book looks at issues concerning poverty and wellbeing, and the role of the government in alleviating poverty in a developed society like the U.S. It is mostly focused on refuting arguments that are used by many politically conservative American Christians to deny a role for government, or to deny the need to help most poor people at all. I also address defenses of the unjust practice of price discrimination, which mostly exacerbates the poverty and distributional problems we face. The section concludes with a consideration of the theology of risk and its implications for practices in the financial markets.

The third group of papers looks at environmental issues. It begins with a study of recycling, addressing why we recycle, objections to the practice, and normative considerations beyond efficiency. The second paper takes up the roles of business, the moral-cultural sector, and government in protecting the environment. The third paper looks at what we can learn from the basic idea of comparative advantage and specialization about the costs of economic development and growth.

The last section of the book contains three studies of globalization. All of them are based on some basic propositions: there are both benefits and costs to globalization, competitive processes in global markets are not determinative of economic outcomes, and we need to carve out the space to make choices about the direction we want globalization to take. We want more out of globalization than just prosperity. We also want to promote ecological sustainability and cultural diversity. Specialization and gains from trade can be useful, but at times they also pose barriers to be overcome.

Though these papers have all been previously published, they have appeared in journals that can be hard to access, especially in smaller college libraries. They are not all indexed in the same place, and so can be difficult to find unless you know exactly what you're looking for. Some are available free on the web, but some only behind pay walls, and some not at all. By bringing them together in this format, I hope this line of research becomes more accessible to Christian academics, clergy, and laypeople, both inside and outside the economics discipline. I think it can provide a useful way of moving forward the discussion of some of the crucial issues of our time.

John P. Tiemstra
Grand Rapids, Michigan
July 2011

Acknowledgments

FOR THE LAST 37 years I have been privileged to serve on the faculty of Calvin College, a large Christian undergraduate college with a well-developed tradition of scholarship, a strong Calvinist intellectual agenda, and many outstanding professors. The beautiful campus is just a bonus. Many colleagues have helped me formulate and think through these ideas, including economists George Monsma, Eugene Dykema, Roland Hoksbergen, Scott Vander Linde, Kurt Schaefer, and others. Outside economics, I have learned much from Nicholas Wolterstorff, Richard Mouw, James K.A. Smith, Shirley Roels, Ronald Wells, George Marsden, Henry Holstege, Douglas Koopmans, Leonard Van Drunen, the late James Penning, the late Edwin Van Kley, and many, many more. Calvin has also supported this work through sabbatical leaves and interim (January) term leaves. When I have taught during interim terms, the students in my reading seminars have also helped me to think through these things.

My major professional affiliations have been with the Association for Social Economics (ASE) and the Association of Christian Economists (ACE). I have been helped in numerous ways by economists Warren Samuels, John B. Davis, Jane Clary, Edward O'Boyle, Andrew Yuengert, Daniel Finn, Charles Wilber, Arnold McKee, the late John Mason, Stephen Smith, James Halteman, David Richardson, John Pisciotta, and many other colleagues and friends I have found through these groups. Participating in professional meetings, regularly reading the association journals, giving papers, and refereeing papers are incredibly valuable experiences that many young scholars today miss because they are reluctant to pay the dues, travel to the meetings, and spend the time. I'm glad I chose to do these things (with Calvin's support), because they made me a much better scholar and writer. I was privileged to serve as the president of ASE, and on the editorial board for ACE, and to receive a lifetime achievement award from ASE.

Permission to reprint the articles in this volume is gratefully acknowledged:

William B. Eerdmans Publishing Company for "Stories Economists Tell," *Reformed Journal* 38(2), pp. 14–16, 1988.

Christian Scholars' Review for "Christianity and Economics: A Review of the Recent Literature," *Christian Scholars' Review* 22(3), pp. 227–47, 1993.

The Association of Christian Economists for "Doing Economics, But Differently," *Bulletin of the Association of Christian Economists* 23, pp. 3–8, 1994.

And for "Poverty, Government, and the Meaning of Economics," *Faith and Economics* 44, pp. 67–77, 2004.

And for "Notes from the Revolution: Principles of a New Economics," *Faith and Economics* 54, pp. 19–29, 2009.

M. E. Sharpe, Inc. for "Why Economists Disagree," *Challenge: the Magazine of Economic Affairs* 41(3), pp. 46–62, 1998. All rights reserved. Not for reproduction.

The Reformed Church in America for "Spiritual Poverty, Material Wealth, Conservative Economics," *Perspectives: A Journal of Reformed Thought* 17(6), pp. 6–9, 2002.

And for "Price Discrimination and Fairness," *Perspectives: A Journal of Reformed Thought* 21(4), pp. 7–12, 2006.

And for "Financial Crisis and the Culture of Risk," *Perspectives: A Journal of Reformed Thought* 24(5), pp.6–10, 2009.

MCB UP Ltd. for "Competitiveness and Industrial Policy," *International Journal of Social Economics* 21(8), pp. 30–42, 1994.

And for "Wasting Time and Wasting the Earth," *International Journal of Social Economics* 29(4), pp. 260–70, 2002.

The Center for Business Ethics at Bentley College for "Environmental Policy for Business and Government," *Business and Society Review* 108(1), pp. 61–9, 2003.

Taylor and Francis for "Rethinking the Costs of Economic Growth," *Review of Social Economy* 66(4), pp. 423–35, 2008.

Springer Verlag for "The Social Economics of Globalization," *Forum for Social Economics* 36(2), pp. 143–59, 2007.

The Association for Religion in Intellectual Life for "Financial Globalization and Crony Capitalism," *CrossCurrents* 56(1), pp. 26–33, 2006.

PART 1

Christian Theology
and Economic Methodology

PART I

1

Stories Economists Tell

THE SWEDISH ACADEMY, IN a display of scrupulous evenhandedness, presented the 1987 Nobel Memorial Prize in Economic Science to arch-liberal American economist Robert M. Solow, a year after giving the 1986 Prize to arch-conservative American economist James Buchanan. This pattern has held for some years now. Thus while Christian economists indulge in fruitless discussions about the advantages of capitalism over socialism, the main event continues to be the debate between Chicago and Cambridge over how to understand and manage a capitalist economy, at least if the Nobel awards have any significance.

It is important for Christians to understand this debate. If we don't, we will permanently lock ourselves out of the intellectual life of the economics profession, with all of its implications for public policy. But more importantly, we are likely to be tempted by the superficial appeal of one or the other position and try to baptize it into our faith. A clear understanding of the conservative/liberal debate in economics will show that a Reformed Christian perspective differs from the main positions the secular world has to offer.

The debate over economics operates on many levels, as most serious and long-standing intellectual disputes do. Economists of Kuyperian leanings have long emphasized the methodological differences at the base of the debate, and the distinctive methodology required for a Christian economics. Other Christian commentators have emphasized the distinctive ethical values Christians bring to this discussion. Without devaluing the importance of methodological and ethical distinctions, I wish to examine another level of this debate.

Conservative and liberal economists have distinctive ways of understanding how society functions. We may call these stories or visions. They are rarely stated explicitly—usually they are shrouded in several layers of higher mathematics. But they inform both the formal theorizing and the policy preferences of the two sides. My contention is that neither the conservative nor the liberal position is consistent with a Christian understanding of a capitalist economy.

Conservatives start with the assumption that people are essentially motivated by self-interested gain-seeking. In particular, the managers of firms in the private business sector are interested in maximizing the profits of their firms, and officials in the public sector are interested in retaining their positions, with all the pay, perquisites, power, and privileges that go with them. Does this kind of behavior serve the public interest? In the business sector, it does. Competition in the marketplace will see to it that business firms that do not give the public what it wants will not make profits, and therefore will fall. Even where there is no actual competition, the threat of new businesses entering the market will guarantee that any firm that does not serve the public's preferences will be supplanted by one that does. On the assumption that individual preferences are the standard for what ought to be done, the public interest is served by this system.

The only monopoly in such a world belongs to the government— the monopoly of the legitimate use of force. The state has power that is unconstrained by market competition. If private interests can enlist this power, they can increase their own financial gains. Any well-financed, well-organized interest group can do this. Such a group can offer public officials valuable resources that can help them get reelected, resources such as money, volunteer labor, and information. They can even offer private-sector jobs to the officials in case they lose their public positions. In exchange for these resources, private groups get public policy that is favorable to their financial interests. By giving government sanction to the exercise of private economic power, this process undercuts market competition. Thus it can never serve the public interest. The general public itself is too disorganized and too diffuse in its interests ever to play a major role in the policy-making process.

There is an internal inconsistency in this position that is worth pointing out. Business firms that are large, profitable, and dominant in their industries have political power by virtue of their dominance and "deep pockets," but they have no economic monopoly because of the constant threat of potential competition for their markets. Monopoly power works in politics, but not in the economy. This paradox leads to a theory in which the most ardent defenders of American capitalism take the strangely Marxist view that the democratic capitalist state serves only the interests of the rich. The theory also offers no hope for reform. There is no reason to expect that a campaign to, say, deregulate the airline industry would ever succeed in the face of self-interested industry opposition. But, of course, that campaign did succeed. The persuasive powers of these conservative economists are more potent than their own theory allows.

Liberal economists start with the same assumptions about human motivation. Firms pursue the maximization of profit, and politicians pursue reelection. Does this kind of behavior serve the public interest? In the business sector, it does not. The tendency is for industries to be dominated by ever fewer and larger firms. These firms will conspire with each other, tacitly or explicitly, to raise prices to monopoly levels. Technology and the actions of businesses serve to deter new competition from entering the market. The consumer loses his sovereignty to the huge enterprises on the economy's commanding heights.

But when it comes to government, the acquisitive instincts of officials are kept in check by competition—the competition of the ballot box. In order to be reelected, and to be able to appoint his cronies to office, a politician must serve the preferences of the voters. If he does not, somebody who does will force him out of office at the next election. This competitive mechanism assures that public policy will serve the public interest, as defined by the preferences of the voters.

The paradox of the liberal approach lies in the assumption that the electorate will favor policies that lead to economic efficiency and growth. For the liberal vision to work, people must vote as consumers, not as producers. They must favor economic policies that mimic the operation of a perfectly competitive market system, even if it means personal sacrifice. The liberal vision fails if, say, the automobile workers secure government protection against imported Japanese cars, fattening their own paychecks while increasing car prices for themselves and everybody else. People have to be more "rational" at the voting booth than they are at the shop.

The liberal and conservative economic schools are close enough to each other that each side recognizes the other as legitimate. Otherwise the comfortable alternation of the Nobel Prize would be much more controversial than it is. Both groups assume that all people are motivated by the self-interested maximization of gain, and both assume that competition will steer self-interested behavior in the direction of the social good defined in terms of individual preferences. But where conservatives claim that minimal government is prerequisite to the achievement of that goal, the liberals would insist that extensive government intervention in the economy is necessary to the public good.

Most theologically conservative Christians are conservative in their economic views as well. Evangelicals seem to have a strong inclination to favor minimal government, and therefore to favor the conservative story about how society works. They see in the Bible a stress on individual responsibility before God, which requires a large degree of individual liberty. They are very aware of the biblical suspicion of the secular "principalities and powers." The idea that market competition naturally keeps sinful impulses in check seems at least consistent with the doctrine of divine providence. Evangelical business people are so convinced that the conservative story is the only truly Christian one that sometimes they are willing to charge those suspected of liberalism with heresy. But many evangelical academic economists buy the conservative story, too (see e.g., Brian Griffiths, *The Creation of Wealth*).

The liberal story also has its adherents among evangelicals (see e.g., Robin Klay, *Counting the Cost*). This group places emphasis on biblical warnings about materialism and on biblical notions of community and "neighborliness." They believe that extensive government intervention in the economy is compatible with personal responsibility toward God in the area of personal morality, and they see the political competition of a democratic society as sufficient to control providentially the sinful impulses of politicians. This is the minority view.

Evangelical Christians who dissent from both sides argue that individual preferences are an inappropriate definition of the public interest (e.g. Hugh James, "Christian Constraints on Capitalism," *Reformed Journal*, May 1987). We would rather see that interest defined in terms of biblically-based standards like stewardship and concern for the poor. In reply, mainstream economists from both camps assert that if stewardship is what the public prefers, that is what the system will give them. Christians need only vote their preferences, along with the rest of society, when they buy goods or elect candidates. But the mainstream theories belie this comforting message. Businesses are never assumed to pursue stewardship, and government leaders are never assumed to have goals beyond reelection. How can either the conservative or the liberal vision of society be correct if people act in any way other than to pursue their own pecuniary gain? Furthermore, how can we assess whether society conforms to the norms of stewardship and justice if unexamined preferences are the standard?

The methodological objection many Christians make to both of these worldviews is that prediction and simplicity are made much too important in assessing these theories (see e.g. Arnold McKee, *Economics and the Christian Mind*). Assuming that people always act in their own self-interest will give one good predictions most of the time. But is that all there is to a good theory? Can we say that these cardboard cut-out gain-seeking individuals reflect the image of God? To have a theory that believing Christians can accept in good conscience, we need an account of human motivation that is complex and rich enough to recognize human beings as moral agents with complicated motives for their actions. Such a theory should give imprecise but accurate predictions. However, it gives up simplicity and ideological neatness in favor of more dearly Christian anthropological foundations.

My main occupation is teaching economics to business students in a Christian college. I am charged to teach students "to lead the Christian life in contemporary society." I need to teach my students that their commitments and values matter to how they behave and to the way the society functions. Neither conservative nor liberal mainstream economics helps me to do that. In the mainstream visions, values and commitments do not matter, because ultimately people simply respond to financial incentives, and societal outcomes are determined by a process of competition. Thus, these visions actually encourage self-interested behavior. As a Christian, I must believe that no matter how sinful we are, our values and commitments do shape our behavior, and God blesses a society that conforms to his will, not our wills.

So, what Christian account of society can I pass along to my students? We all have our own vision of a good society, of what constitutes the public interest. Those visions may be self-centered, but more likely, if we are serious about being Christian, they are based on religious or secular ethical norms. People act on the basis of their visions. The choices of a vocation, a home, and social and political affiliations are based on a person's conception of the public good. That conception also guides a person's daily policies and activities, including the decisions made by business managers and political officials. To understand how a particular society functions and how particular decisions are made, we must understand the commitments and visions of the people involved.

If behavior appears to be self-interested, that may simply be the result of the consistency of people's choice of a position in society with their social vision. People who choose to go into business, for example, tend to be people who believe that business is an important social institution. It is entirely consistent for such people to act politically to ensure the continued viability and legitimacy of the social institution of business. If such people advocate government regulation of business, it will very likely be because they believe that additional accountability of business to the public is needed to preserve business legitimacy, and not just because they might expect to profit from regulation. If politicians favor protectionism, or business managers act to limit competitive rivalry, the reason may lie less in a desire for reelection or for profit than in an underlying belief that a good society offers stability in people's lives and not just ever-growing amounts of economic goods.

Competition plays a very different role in this vision than it does in mainstream economics. For both liberal and conservative mainstream economists, competition is an unmitigated good. But in this Christian vision, competition is a mixed blessing. Competition prods people to do their best, but so does an attitude of conscientious service to God and neighbor. Competition promotes instability, arouses jealousy, and can provide incentives for immoral behavior. People instinctively avoid competition not just in an effort to increase their own economic and political power, but also to promote stability and cooperation. Hence it is a less powerful force in society than mainstream stories suggest. Competition is not necessary to achieve the public good, nor is it always even desirable.

Those of us who tell this alternative Christian story are often accused of being liberals, especially by those evangelicals who accept the conventional conservative story. This is an understandable mistake. We are often critical of the performance of the private business sector, where individual self-interest tends to run amok. We sometimes recommend government intervention in the economy, which in our view is not necessarily a bad thing. But true liberals have given up entirely on the private sector, and focus most of their attention on "optimal" public policy. We believe that private business policy matters, too, and can be shaped by changing visions of the role of business in promoting the public good. That is why I am glad to see my students go into business. I believe that their Christian commitment and education can make a difference to society.

This is an untidy vision. It does not always offer clear predictions, and it requires a lot of work in discovering people's motivations. It does not offer an unambiguous definition of the public interest, and it does not point to a single set of social arrangements that guarantee the achievement of the public good. But it does set an important task for the Christian community. As pastors and educators, we can offer our constituents a dearer and richer understanding of the workings of our society. We can help people define for themselves a vision of a good society that conforms to biblical Christian principles. We can tell leaders in both business and government that their values matter and urge them to act out their Christian commitment in their professional lives. A Christian economic story can help us to make a little more real the old Reformed concept of the transformation of society to conform to the will of God.

REFERENCES

Griffiths, Brian. 1984. *The Creation of Wealth: A Christian's Case for Capitalism.* Downers Grove, IL: InterVarsity.

James, Hugh. 1987. "Christian Constraints on Capitalism." *Reformed Journal* 37(5).

Klay, Robin Kendrick. 1986. *Counting the Cost: The Economics of Christian Stewardship.* Grand Rapids: Eerdmans.

McKee, Arnold F. 1987. *Economics and the Christian Mind: Elements of a Christian Approach to the Economy and Economic Science.* New York: Vantage.

2

Christianity and Economics
A Review of the Recent Literature

THE LAST FIFTEEN YEARS have seen an explosion of work written by American evangelicals concerning the relationship of faith and learning in the field of economics. Enough has now appeared that some patterns can be discerned, and some generalizations drawn. The recent review of this literature by Craig Gay [1991] offers a more extensive summary than can be essayed here, but his perspective is the sociology of religion. The categories of this essay will be those of an economist. After reviewing the biblical foundations for Christian concern about the economy, and the much-debated question of socialism, this essay will turn to the dual critique of mainstream economics that is offered by Christians. The institutionalist response to that critique will then be considered. Along the way, comments will be offered evaluating the state of the discussion. It is hoped that this essay can become a useful "reader's guide" to this extensive literature, as well as offering some direction for future investigation. Scholars from other disciplines may also find this review to be useful as an example of the way the faith and learning discussion might proceed.

BIBLICAL FOUNDATIONS

In many fields the faith and learning debate is plagued by disagreement over the interpretation and status of the relevant biblical material. The debate over "creation science" is a prominent example. Therefore it is remarkable that the faith and economics literature exhibits a high degree of consensus on the basic biblical principles that inform the analysis. Though there are many statements of these basic principles [see Barnett, 1987; Haan, 1988; Hay, 1989, ch. 1; Meeks, 1989; Mott, 1987; National Conference, 1986, ch. 2; North, 1973; Sider, 1980b; 1990, chs. 3 and 4; Tiemstra, 1990, ch. 5; Wolterstorff, 1987; for some of the more explicit statements], they can be expressed briefly:

Stewardship

God is the owner of all wealth and humans are his stewards or trustees. It is this principle that gives relevance to the consideration of a specifically Christian approach to economic activity. The breadth of its acceptance accounts for the willingness of Christians from many theological traditions, even the more pietist and separatist ones, to consider an integrated Christian approach.

Poverty

There is a clear obligation for believers to see to the needs of the poor. It may come as a surprise to the reader that both politically liberal and conservative evangelicals accept this basic biblical idea, since secular conservative social commentary often displays little concern for the poor. But the problem of poverty is a prominent feature of the Christianity and economics literature. Needless to say there is a great deal of disagreement over the nature and causes of poverty, possible solutions, and the appropriate locus of assistance to the poor.

Materialism

While the Bible makes it clear that wealth is not a bad thing in itself, and may indeed be a blessing from God, placing hope and trust in material prosperity is a form of idolatry, and hence is inappropriate for believers.

The range of opinion here goes from a liberal suspicion of all gain-seeking behavior, to conservative endorsement of the old Wesleyan injunction to "work all you can, earn all you can, and give all you can."

Work

Work is the appropriate Christian response to the cultural mandate, and people ordinarily ought to support themselves by working. Again, the causes and solutions of unemployment are the sources of much disagreement, but the importance of work is universally accepted.

Areas of Disagreement

Biblical notions of justice and the proper role of the state provoke the major disagreements among these writers. Some, like Sider [1990], hold that care for the poor is a matter of justice, and therefore calls for a significant government role. On the other side, writers like Beisner [1988] believe that biblical justice only involves fairness in economic transactions and equality before the law, precluding a redistributive role for government. It seems that writers from both sides read into the biblical material ideas from modern political theory. This issue is unlikely to be settled by appeal to the Bible alone.

THE QUESTION OF ECONOMIC SYSTEMS

A quick survey of the titles in the bibliography will give the (correct) impression that much of this literature explicitly addresses the question of whether capitalism or socialism is more acceptable to Christians, with the majority of these works propounding a defense of capitalism along politically and socially conservative lines [Beisner, 1988; Boersema, 1983, 1986; Gay, 1991, Epilogue; Lindsell, 1982; Nash, 1986; North, 1973; Schaeffer, 1985]. In my view, this focus on the question of economic systems has unfortunately diverted the discussion from some more important issues. But before considering whether the debate over systems has been productive, we must consider how the literature came to take this turn.

Christian Advocates of Socialism

If we stick to the economists' common definition of socialism, i.e., government ownership of the means of production, it is very difficult to find any serious Christian socialists. The most prominent would be a few of the most famous mid-century mainline Protestant theologians, and some contemporary Latin American Catholic practitioners of liberation theology. Paul Tillich certainly qualifies, as does Karl Barth, and perhaps the early Reinhold Niebuhr. The most prominent liberation theologians would be Jose Miguez-Bonino and Gustavo Gutierrez. But the theological distance between these thinkers and the evangelical writers considered here is quite great, and a debate between them would have to be considered a footnote to the modernist-fundamentalist controversy. Less importantly, of all these socialist theologians, only Niebuhr was born in the U.S., and he recanted his socialism. So the relevance of such a debate to the U.S. context would be questionable.

The history of Christian socialism through the centuries is well told by the American Catholic scholar John C. Cort [1988], who identifies himself as a socialist. Though an advocate of worker cooperatives, Cort is opposed to the nationalization of industry, and hence is not a socialist by the usual definition. (A less sympathetic history is Preston [1986].) Andrew Kirk [1983] would seem to be the main evangelical socialist, to judge by citations in the procapitalist writings. But Kirk's socialism is limited to the nationalization of railroads, telephones, and some natural resources, which is virtually universal outside the U.S. This may be partly explained by the fact that Kirk is British. To find an advocate for socialism to include as one of his "four Christian views," Clouse [1984] also had to go to the old country and find a theologian, John Gladwin. Lutz [1987] found a black South African Lutheran, Sibusiso Bengu, to represent the socialist position. Philip Wogaman ventured a tentative preference for some form of socialism in his earlier work [1977, p. 158], but when he fills out his views [1986], they seem similar to those of Cort. The conclusion is hard to escape: there are no American evangelical socialists. That side of the "debate" does not exist.

The Fundamental Confusion

This focus on a debate over capitalism has had two unfortunate effects: it has obscured the true issues, and it has detached the evangelical literature from the larger debate over public policy and economics.

The critical voices in the evangelical literature on economics have not aimed their criticism at capitalism as a system. Rather, the majority of them are concerned primarily about the direction of policy and behavior at all levels of society. They are critical of American families for being too self-centered and materialistic. They are critical of business for being insensitive to the needs of their various constituencies. And they are critical of government for priorities that seem misplaced when compared to the biblical principles. The issue is not whether we shall have capitalism or socialism, but rather, how should we act out our roles as consumers, workers, managers, statesmen, and voters in a democratic capitalist society.

As an example, take the famous work of Ronald Sider [1990], against which much of the conservative literature is aimed. Sider does not advocate socialism in his book. He is, however, very critical of business for alleged abuses of its power, particularly the role of multinational corporations in the Third World. He is critical of American consumers, especially Christians, for their preoccupation with their material standard of living. His most controversial recommendation is that American Christians limit their standard of living voluntarily, and adopt a "graduated tithe." He is critical of the U.S. government for policies based on the ultimate priority of American prosperity and international power, rather than self-determination, human rights, and sustenance for the majority of the world's population. But his recommendation is similarly modest: adoption of the United Nations' program for reforming world trade and increasing the flow of aid to the poor countries. Sider's advocacy of a redistributive role for the state is probably the source of the accusation that he is socialist, but there are many non-socialists who share this view. Now, all of this is controversial, and should be the subject of vigorous discussion within the Christian community. The quality of analysis in Sider's book, especially in the earlier editions, was not especially good, and deserved some criticism [Tiemstra, 1979]. But shifting the conversation to an altogether different level by interpreting Sider's work as an attack on capitalism only obscured and confused an important issue.

Some of the writers have very explicitly made neoclassical economic theory the object of their criticism [Cramp, 1975, 1983; Hay, 1989; McKee, 1987; Storkey, 1986; Tiemstra, 1990; Vickers, 1976, 1982; Wilber and

Jameson, 1983, 1990]. The point here is not that capitalism is not a good system, but rather that the account of the workings of capitalism offered by neoclassical theory is not a good account. The confusion of the would-be defenders of capitalism in this case is to identify the theory with the system, so that an attack on one is held to be an attack on the other. To a point, this is understandable. The fundamental theorem of neoclassical welfare economics, which holds that a perfectly competitive market economy will, under certain conditions, produce a Pareto-optimal allocation of resources, is often used as the centerpiece of a defense of capitalism as a system. But the neoclassical defense is not the only possible defense of capitalism, and in fact, few of the Christian defenders use it. Moving the discussion to the level of systems has obscured and confused the very important debate about theories.

By focusing on a debate over systems, evangelical writers have re-moved the literature on Christianity and economics far from the main-stream of political discussion. For whatever reason, there has never been a substantial socialist movement in the United States. No socialist party has ever attracted much attention or many votes. The labor movement in the U.S. has been very conservative in its political attitudes. While it has supported the expansion of welfare programs and social insurance, it has never advocated nationalization, and has been virulently anti-communist on foreign policy. The national press and the mainstream political journals simply ignore socialism as an issue. While there have always been com-plaints about Marxist scholars in the universities, they have always been a minority in every field, and a very small minority in economics. All of this was true even before the Revolution of 1989, which made support for state ownership of industry and central planning unthinkable even in Europe. Any outsider observing the great concern over socialism among evangeli-cal Christians must wonder what planet these people come from.

All of this suggests that Craig Gay [1991] is incorrect when he invokes the "new class" hypothesis to explain the positions taken in this literature. If evangelicals wanted to adopt the agenda of the new class in order to legiti-mate their own role as social critics, they would not have made capitalism versus socialism the putative focus of their writings. The new class buried that issue a long time ago. Nor would as many evangelical economists have gone out of their way to be highly critical of the neoclassical mainstream. There is very little prestige, money, or influence to be found outside the mainstream of the economics profession. In fact, there isn't even much company to be found there. At the Christmas meetings of the Allied Social Science Associations, the explicitly Christian groups like the Association of Christian Economists and the Association for Social Economics (a predominantly Catholic group) are assigned to very small rooms.

The Area of Consensus

There seems to be a consensus that a modest defense of capitalism is appropriate for Christians. Democratic capitalism is not the kingdom of God, as Novak [1982, p. 28] puts it. Indeed, it would be inappropriate to claim that any economic system is uniquely Christian [Barnett, 1987, ch. 13; Heyne, 1990; Pierard, 1989; Ellul, 1984; Waterman, 1985]. But a twofold defense can be offered.

To begin with, capitalism works pretty well. Market economies are not plagued with shortages of goods, as are modem socialist economies (the ones that still exist). In democratic capitalist societies, the middle class has expanded significantly, so that average people are not poor, and prosperity is common. The third-world countries that have reached "middle-income" status have done so on the basis of market capitalist institutions, though each has its own policy variations. Though there is nothing in economic theory or economic history to suggest that a capitalist system on its own will eliminate poverty, many· democratic capitalist societies have virtually eliminated poverty with the help of relatively unintrusive government policies. Thus, pragmatic considerations favor capitalism.

The institution of private ownership seems to allow greater scope for the exercise of stewardship than state ownership. State ownership removes the responsibility for care in the use of resources to a level of bureaucracy far beyond the everyday concerns of those who are most intimately involved in the enterprise, even when the governmental institutions are democratic. Here again, the case must be largely pragmatic, and not principial, because many capitalist economies suffer from excessive concentration of wealth and the existence of excessively large, bureaucratized private businesses. For the ideal of stewardship to be realized, ownership must be widely distributed [Smedes, 1965; Speiser, 1989]. A democratic capitalist society at least does not foreclose this possibility, and with appropriate policies may achieve it.

THE ETHICAL CRITIQUE OF NEOCLASSICAL ECONOMICS

Secular Antecedents

Neoclassical economic theory is founded on nineteenth century British utilitarian philosophy. Indeed, the influence of Jeremy Bentham and John Stuart Mill continues to pervade the discipline. But the problems of utilitarianism have long been recognized by economists, and some of the bolder ones have pointed to these problems in print. The neoclassical account of individual decision-making, with its emphasis on self-interested, gain-seeking behavior, does a poor job of accounting for the normative and affective factors that influence human decisions, even in economic matters [Etzioni, 1988]. The neoclassical pretense that a normative or welfare economics can be value-free, based entirely on objectively rational principles, cannot be sustained. The practical and philosophical problems with neoclassical welfare economics are numerous and basic [Little, 1962]. The difficulties with economic growth as the ultimate objective of economic activity and policy began to be appreciated as a result of the commodity price explosion and the rise of the environmental movement in the 1970s [Mishan, 1967; Hirsch, 1977]. Beginning in that decade, Christian economists built an ethical critique of the neoclassical school on these foundations.

A Statement of the Ethical Critique

Neoclassical welfare economics, by taking as its normative standard the greatest good for the greatest number, and by taking good to mean self-perceived happiness derived from economic consumption, adopts an ethic that is foreign to biblical Christianity. The desires of individuals are infected with the sinfulness that we all inherit as part of our nature, and hence are an inadequate ethical foundation for economic policy. The individualistic and materialistic assumptions of this theory neglect dimensions of welfare that are connected to the community and to non-material standards. Welfare economics overemphasizes allocation questions and underemphasizes distribution questions, which by biblical standards are more important. [Cramp, 1983, ch. 3; Daly and Cobb, 1989, ch. 2; Dykema, 1989; Hay, 1989, ch. 3; Goudzwaard, 1979, ch. 13; McKee, 1987, ch. 9; Tiemstra, 1990, ch. 2; Vickers, 1982, pt. 1; Wauzzinski, 1989]

Biblical principles do not support economic growth as the ultimate goal of society. The notion that growth is always a good thing is based on the materialistic principle that more is always better, which is clearly unbiblical. The negative consequences of growth in measured output—pollution, congestion, resource depletion, and the fragmentation of life—conflict with the principle of stewardship. And in a rich society like the U.S. growth is neither a necessary nor sufficient condition for the elimination of poverty. [Daly and Cobb, 1989, ch. 3; Hoksbergen, 1983; Goudzwaard, 1974,1979; Cramp, 1983, ch. 6; Hay, 1989, ch. 8; Lee, 1981; McCullum, 1977; Monsma, 1980; Rasmussen, 1981, ch. 7; Sider, 1990, ch. 2; Stivers, 1976; Taylor, 1975, ch. 1; Tiemstra, 1990, ch. 13; Vandezande, 1984; Wilber and Jameson, 1982]

The neoclassical account of self-interested, gain-seeking individuals is incapable of describing the behavior of Christians who are trying to live according to the stewardship principle. Furthermore, since all humans are created in the image of God, and hence are by their very nature religious and moral beings, the neoclassical model fails to capture an essential dimension of human behavior. [Cramp, 1975, sec. C; Daly and Cobb, 1989, ch. 4; Dykema, 1989; Hay, 1989, ch. 3; Tiemstra, 1990, ch. 2; Richardson, 1981.]

By teaching people the utilitarian ideology of neoclassical economics, economists encourage the very kind of self-interested, greedy behavior that is inconsistent with the demands of the Christian life and destructive to the economy itself. [Daly and Cobb, 1989, pp. 50–51; Griffiths, 1984, ch. 5; Hay, 1989, ch. 4; Hill, 1987; Mullin, 1984, ch. 10; Rasmussen, 1981, chs. 3 and 4; Taylor, 1973, ch. I)

Responses to the Ethical Critique

A number of Christian economists, operating with the conventional positive/normative distinction, make the case that textbook economics merely tells how the world works, and can be put in the service of any values the policymaker wants to achieve. [Klay, 1986, ch. 1; Beckmann, 1981; Copeland, 1988; Diehl, 1984; Catherwood, 1983; Kreider, 1984; Owensby, 1988) Values are added on after the analysis has been done in order to point the way for policy recommendations, usually aimed at government. These authors propose Christian values that the economy should serve, and then recommend "economically efficient" policies to achieve those objectives.

This approach is vulnerable to the methodological critique, posited below, which denies the existence of a positive/ normative distinction in economic theory. Furthermore, it conceives of economics as an analytical engine for generating government policies, which can always fix up market failures that result in undesirable outcomes. The impact of the approach is undermined by the political difficulty of implementing efficient policies and problems of "government failure." Some of these writers do occasionally address policy recommendations to individuals and businesses, but it is unclear how the behavior they recommend can be consistent with the theories of household and business behavior at their base.

Halteman [1988] argues for a two-kingdom approach to economics. While believers are held to high standards for their economic behavior, including a high level of concern for the interests of others, unbelievers are unlikely to practice such behavior. Neoclassical theory, then, can serve as an adequate description of the behavior of worldly people, and of the economy that they dominate. The economics of the Bible applies only to communities of believers who have organized themselves into economic units. Gish's "decentralist economics" [1984] is of the same type, as is the approach of Yoder [1986]. A similar approach, based on Catholic traditions, seems to inform the work of Pemberton and Finn [1985].

Halteman's sharp distinction between Christians and the world comes out of his frankly anabaptist worldview. Pemberton and Finn draw on similar strains that come from the monastic tradition of Catholicism. For writers of Calvinist persuasion, this view gives up too easily any influence that Christians may have on the broader society in which they live, and is too quick to counsel believers to withdraw to a self-contained world of their own making. This view also makes too sharp a distinction between the human nature of believers and unbelievers. Of course, believers do not immediately shed all the effects of sin in their lives, and hence may continue to let improper self-interest motivate them. But more important, Calvinists insist on the religious nature of all persons. Even unbelievers have their own faith commitments, which inform their economic decisions. Unless they are all committed to the same utilitarian hedonism, neoclassical economics will continue to fail to account for their behavior.

Nash [1989} is an advocate for Austrian school economics, which he claims answers the ethical critique. According to Nash, the Austrians claim that behavior in the marketplace simply reflects the subjective valuations placed on goods by individuals, without trying to characterize the sources of those valuations. Theologians and moralists may criticize particular choices on religious or moral grounds, but that has nothing to do with economic theory. Indeed, he claims that Austrian theory can account for the influence of non-material values on economic behavior better than the neoclassical school can.

Austrian economics has proven attractive to many evangelical thinkers, but it has problems of its own. As will be noted below, this type of theory has even more methodological problems than neoclassical theory does. But as far as ethical foundations are concerned the troubling aspect of Austrian thinking is its tendency to judge all social arrangements on the basis of the degree of liberty they allow to individual participants. If liberty were the only Christian social principle, or even the most important one, the Austrian position would be a much more comfortable one for Christians to take. But the neglect of biblical values concerning poverty, work, stewardship, and materialism makes Austrian economics unattractive to most proponents of the ethical critique.

A similar response comes from those eager to save the neoclassical approach whole. For example, Novak [1982, ch. 4] claims that the ethical critique misconstrues the neoclassical use of the concept of "self-interest." Self-interest merely refers to whatever interest a self might have, whether greedy or noble. He quotes a famous passage from Milton Friedman to the effect that "Self-interest is not myopic selfishness. It is whatever it is that interests the participants, whatever they value, whatever goals they pursue" (p. 94). Similarly, Richardson [1988] claims that the neoclassical notion of utility-maximization is flexible enough to accommodate all kinds of motivations-the classic "black box." He praises the so-called "new institutional" economics for exploiting this flexibility by introducing more realism into assumptions about economic actors' motivations.

It is no doubt true that as a mathematical construct, neoclassical theory is a wonderfully flexible instrument. But, contrary to the belief of some, neoclassical economics is not just a mathematical construct. To qualify as economics, interpretation has to be given to mathematical models. In the mainstream journals and books, that interpretation is inevitably based on self-interested, no, selfish, hedonistic, economic man. Though Friedman defends the openness of neoclassical theory in his popular writings, I have never found a professional paper of his that explores the behavior of a household that is not hedonistic or a firm that does not maximize profits. It is not clear that the ideological conclusions that he reaches—the necessity of limited government, the achievement of low inflation by control of the money supply—would survive such a reinterpretation of his models. Though the new "institutionalists" have renewed interest in the particulars of economic structure, they have done so mainly by pushing the assumption of "economic man" to a lower level in the hierarchy of the firm. Instead of the firm as a profit-maximizing black box, it becomes an organized collection of human utility-maximizing black boxes. The ethical critique still applies.

The desirability of economic growth is the subject of a recent work by Beisner [1990]. He claims that the Cultural Mandate is a warrant for both economic and population growth. Drawing on the economics of Julian Simon, he claims that this growth can be accomplished without creating the kinds of problems posited in the ethical critique, and that it is in fact demanded by a proper understanding of the notion of stewardship.

The discussion of economic growth can easily become confused, because different people have different ideas about the direction and nature of future growth. Economic growth never means just more of the same old goods. Technological change means that the goods themselves change, and the direction of that change is difficult to predict. We need less abstract discussion about the desirability of growth, and more discussion of the role and direction of research and development activity, and the concrete social improvements that we have in mind when we talk about growth. Beisner is clearly too optimistic about growth, especially when discussing pollution. The critics are probably too pessimistic, though if read carefully, their claims are rather modest. Two very helpful works on this topic that have come out of the Calvin Center for Christian Scholarship are Wilkinson [1980] and Monsma [1986].

Novak's observation that a vigorous moral-cultural system is indispensable in a democratic capitalist society [1982, pp. 182–86] seems at first to confirm the critics' point that the institutions of religion, education, and journalism have been coopted by utilitarian ideology. He takes the opposite view, however. He argues that the moral-cultural institutions have been too critical of the capitalist economy and the supporting ideology, and that this threatens the health of the whole society. In his view, the schools, churches, and journals should do more to reinforce the ideology of democratic capitalism as it is set forth in neoclassical theory.

Novak seems caught in a dilemma here. The moral-cultural sector is needed to provide a check on the abuses of capitalism, but it is also needed to buttress the utilitarian faith in markets. Presumably some kind of balance is called for. That the moral-cultural institutions come under attack from both sides may be an indication that the balance has been struck appropriately. The issue seems to demand some empirical investigation, though that may not settle the issue. Benne's account [1981] of democratic capitalism is similar to Novak's, but Benne perceives a need for greater control of the market by the moral-cultural forces. The most serious gap in Novak's analysis is his failure to suggest a theory about how the moral-cultural sector influences decision-making in the economy. Such a theory is necessary to his view of how democratic capitalism functions, and that theory is not provided within the neoclassical paradigm. As shall be noted below, the institutionalist alternative fills this gap.

THE METHODOLOGICAL CRITIQUE OF NEOCLASSICAL ECONOMICS

Philosophical Antecedents

That there are problems with economic methodology has been known for a long time. For many years it was the standard practice for the presidents of the American Economic Association and its British counterpart, after long and distinguished mainstream careers, to devote their presidential addresses to the criticism of mainstream methodology. (A famous example is Harrod [1938].) None of this had very much impact until it was abundantly clear that the consensus on the philosophy of science had completely broken down. This breakdown worked its way into economists' consciousness through a series of extended works on economic methodology that appeared in the early and middle 1980s [Blaug, 1980; Caldwell, 1982; Boland, 1982; McCloskey, 1985; Mirowski, 1988]. The conclusion that most economists seemed to draw from all of this ferment was not that neoclassical economics was hopelessly flawed, but rather that methodology was a kind of free-for-all, Since no consensus existed, any and every methodology was valid, and the main point was to be persuasive. Since most of the practitioners were persuaded by the neoclassical paradigm to begin with, very little changed in the way economics is actually done. The conservative political climate of the time made the status quo that much more irresistible.

The collapse of philosophical foundationalism and the destruction of the consensus about science left the way open for self-consciously Christian philosophers to propose their own approach to epistemology and the philosophy of science. [Wolterstorff, 1984; Plantinga, 1990; Van Leeuwen, 1982] The essence of this approach is that if our theology, our faith, and our experience as Christians have anything to teach us about everyday matters like science and society, we should use that knowledge in constructing theories about the world around us. Otherwise, we are doing our scholarship and research with one eye closed and one hand tied behind our back. We don't know enough about the world to shut out any of the knowledge we have, even if that knowledge is inextricably related to our spiritual experience. To do otherwise is to deny the lordship of Christ over all of life, by denying him access to the world of scholarship. This methodological approach opens up the possibility of a distinctively and uniquely Christian scholarship, but at the very least it suggests that theories ought to be accepted as useful only if they comport well with our Christian commitment.

A Statement of the Methodological Critique

Neoclassical economists are incorrect when they claim that "positive" (i.e., descriptive) economics is value-free, and that therefore values only enter into "normative" (i.e., prescriptive) economics. Value judgments are inevitably involved in deciding which questions to study, which data are relevant, which theory to select of the infinite number that are consistent with the data, and which method to use to validate the theory. The value judgments that neoclassical economics reflects are often at odds with biblical principles and priorities. [Cramp, 1983, chs. 1 and 4; Daly and Cobb, 1989, pp. 130–132; Goudzwaard, 1979, ch. 19, 1986; McKee, 1987, ch. 7; Rasmussen, 1981, ch. 2; Shinn, 1985; Storkey, 1986, ch. 2; Tiemstra, 1990, ch. 3].

By accepting as data only observed economic behavior, and not introspective reports concerning motives, values, and the like, economists have cut themselves off from an important source of information. Simply assuming that behavior is somehow "self-interested" gives no clue about how that behavior might change in response to changes in social and political conditions or changes in philosophies and values. [Cramp, 1983, ch. 2; Hay, 1989, ch. 3; Tiemstra, 1990, ch. 3; McKee, 1987, ch. 8; Vickers, 1976, ch. 2]

Neoclassical economics often puts much too high a premium on mathematical sophistication and logical rigor, partly as a result of the attempt to expunge values from positive theory. The result is theories that are aesthetically very pleasing, but have little or no connection to real-world phenomena. Rigorous interpretation of these mathematical models often results in mere tautologies that are useless as theory. To be sure, theories should be logically consistent, but not to the exclusion of information from a Christian philosophical anthropology. Though the mainstream has a real problem with this, it applies even more to Austrian School economics, which appears to pursue abstraction and logical rigor to the exclusion of all other criteria for theory selection. [Beversluis, 1982; Daly and Cobb, 1989, pp. 35–41; McKee, 1987, ch. 8; Tiemstra, 1990, ch. 4; Van Dahm, 1986]

Responses to the Methodological Critique

Elzinga [1981] classifies five possible approaches to the integration of faith and learning in economics: the mainstream Christian economist, an economist who happens to be a Christian; the Christian political economist, who looks for certain economic outcomes based on Christian values, but uses conventional analysis to determine how to reach them; the economic reformist, who looks for a distinctively Christian economic science; the applied Christian economist, who offers practical economic advice to Christians; and the church economist, who is interested in the economic behavior of the Christian community. Elzinga claims that valuable contributions can be made by economists from all five of these perspectives. He thus appears to endorse the methodological pluralism that became popular in the discipline in the 1980s. The position he is most dubious about is the economic reformist, and the source of his doubts appears to be a strict form of the positive/normative distinction. He states, "The Christian economist might fault the secular economist, who purports to do positive economics but falls an unwary victim to all sorts of normative presuppositions. Yet the Christian economist might at the same time be prone to impose his or her worldview upon Christian economics" (p. 16). A little further on he states that this bias will come in at the level of hermeneutics, rather than the level of political ideology.

By adopting the positive/normative distinction without comment, Elzinga leaves himself vulnerable to the methodological critique without answering it. The critique asserts that a value free positive economics is impossible, so at least the values that are at the foundation of our economics ought to be Christian ones. Elzinga is correct that no one interpretation of those values will command unanimous consent. As we have already noted, economics done by Calvinists looks different from that done by anabaptists or fundamentalists. But why should Christians accept an economics based on non-Christian value judgments, especially if methodological pluralism is acceptable? Furthermore, there does seem to be a large area of consensus concerning the biblical principles for economics, as noted above. Should we not try to build on this consensus?

Nash [1986] asserts that "There is no such thing as positive Christian economics. The distinction that counts is between good and bad economics" (p. 12). As his language suggests, he also operates with a strong positive/normative distinction. While he does not claim in so many words that positive economics is value-free, he does assert that positive economic claims can be easily settled by appeal to the data. Questions of the nature or interpretation of data are ignored. Nash seems to take Austrian theory to be more or less self-evidently true. While most of the book is unabashedly normative, Nash does not draw any contrast between the focus on individual liberty at the basis of the Austrian school, and the focus on stewardship that characterizes Christian thought on economics. Olasky et al [1989] extend this approach to development economics.

Nash does not really try to answer the critics of the Austrian school methodology. It is something of a puzzle that people who hold a minority position in a discipline, as Austrian economics surely is, can assert so confidently that the data show them to be plainly and unequivocally right. If that were the case, would not the majority have come over to their side long since? The fact that multiple schools continue to exist in economics is prima facie evidence that the data by themselves do not settle anything. The differences continue to exist because of differences in the philosophical positions economists hold. And for that reason, if no other, we should not expect that any Christian approach to economics would ever achieve consensus status, or even majority assent.

THE INSTITUTIONALIST ALTERNATIVE

Four Antecedents

Some Christian scholars who accept the validity of the dual critique of neoclassical economics have opted for an alternative approach that is generally described as institutionalism. There are four strains of economic thinking that contribute to this alternative position.

Institutionalist economics per se is a school of thought that began with the turn-of-the-century American economists Thorstein Veblen and John R. Commons. The best-known recent contributor to this school is John Kenneth Galbraith, whose wit, style, and political influence have made his books popular with a general audience well beyond his influence within the economics profession. This school focuses on traditional and institutional constraints on economic decision-making and the institutional nature of economic transactions, with stress on the unequal power of economic agents. At its best, it also tries to account for the variety of human motivation in economic decisions. The content of institutionalist theory can vary enormously depending on the questions under investigation. Current institutionalist work appears in the *Journal of Economic Issues* (published in the U.S. by the Association for Evolutionary Economics) and the *Review of Political Economy* (published in the U.K.).

Post-Keynesian economics was founded by a number of the associates of John Maynard Keynes at Cambridge University, and is sometimes referred to as the "Cambridge School." Early proponents include Joan Robinson, Richard Stone (Nobel laureate), and Nicholas Kaldor. Current representatives include Paul Davidson and the Christian economist Douglas Vickers, who wrote the only post-Keynesian money and banking textbook [1985]. Rather than search for neoclassical micro foundations for Keynesian macro theory, this school is dedicated to elaborating a micro theory that is implied by Keynes's macro insights. This theory stresses a number of institutionalist elements, including imperfect competition, inflexible institutions, and alternative motivations. Current work appears in the *Journal of Post-Keynesian Economics* (U.S.) and the *Cambridge Journal of Economics* (U.K.).

Social economics is a school of thought that takes as its basis concern what was once called "the social question." It is strongly oriented toward elaborating the economic implications of Catholic social thought, and its founder was the German Catholic economist Heinrich Pesch. Current writers in this tradition include William Waters and William Dugger, both associated with DePaul University in Chicago. The main distinction between social economics and the neoclassical school seems to be the use of Catholic rather than utilitarian values for the selection of research questions and the evaluation of economic institutions and policies. However, it must be said that there is not a well-defined social economic theory, and many social economists are also institutionalists or post-Keynesians.

Current work appears in the *Review of Social Economy* (published in the U.S. by the Association for Social Economics) and the *International Journal of Social Economics* (U.K.).

Discontent with neoclassical theories of economic development and the depressing circumstances of the Third World in the 1960s and 1970s led to the development of new theories that draw on institutionalist ideas like imperfect competition and the role of inequality of economic and political power in determining economic outcomes. Leaders of this school included Gunnar Myrdal (Nobel laureate), Raul Prebish, Paul Streeten, and Immanuel Wallerstein. Current work appears in *World Development.*

Christian Proponents of Institutionalism

The Christian thinkers who have taken the lead in developing the dual critique are for the most part the same ones identified with one or another of the various strains of institutionalism. Classical institutionalism is present in Cramp [1975, 1983], Goudzwaard [1975, 1979], Storkey [1979], Speiser [1989], Stivers [1989], Tiemstra [1988, 1990], and Wauzzinski [1989]. The post-Keynesian perspective is quite clear in the works of Daly and Cobb [1989], Haan [1971], Vickers [1976, 1982, 1985] (as noted above), Storkey [1986], Wilber and Jameson [1983, 1990], and Tiemstra [1990]. Social economics appears mostly in the works of some of the Catholic writers: McKee [1987], National Conference of Catholic Bishops [1986], Pemberton and Finn [1985], Wilber and Hoksbergen [1986], and Williams [1982, 1987]. A great many Christian writers have shown an interest in the less-conventional development theories, partly because of the great emphasis on missions and overseas development work in the churches. They include Antonides [1978], Beals [1985], Byron [1982], Duchrow [1987], Elliott [1987], Goulet [1982], Jegen and Manno [1978], Jegen and Wilber [1979], Mieth and Pohier [1980], National Conference [1986, ch. 3], Sider [1980a, 1990], Simon [1984], and Wolterstorff [1983].

Almost without exception, these writers are either Calvinists or Catholics. The few Lutherans and other mainline Protestants who make the list are mostly concerned about development issues. It is the Calvinist and some parts of the Catholic traditions that have historically been most concerned about the problem of living out the Christian life in society, rather than being somehow separate from the secular world. It is also these traditions that have been the most concerned about social reform in the name of Christian principles, and who have placed the most stress on Christian academic education at all levels. Christian writers from other traditions have been less willing, and perhaps less well equipped, to propose an alternative to secular orthodoxy in the field of economics, with all its academic and practical implications. It is undoubtedly the different approaches to the "Christianity and culture" problem that these traditions have historically taken [Niebuhr, 1951] that account for their different approaches to economics, rather than the class identifications proposed by Gay [1991].

Why Institutionalism?

Institutionalism was not developed in the first place by scholars concerned with the faith-and-Iearning problem—it is not a uniquely Christian theory. The Christian writers who have adopted it for their own work have generally not offered an elaborate justification for choosing it. But it seems clear that the basic reason it is preferred by these Calvinist and Catholic scholars has to do with the fact that, at least in some of its forms, it is not vulnerable to the dual critique. Furthermore, it does not have some of the intellectual and ideological problems of other possible alternatives, notably Marxism.

Institutionalist approaches allow economists to focus on objectives for society other than efficiency in the allocation of resources and maximization of economic growth. Such concerns as care for the environment, equity in the distribution of income, quality of work life, social cohesion, a high moral climate, richness of mediating institutions, and cultural richness, among others, can become the focus of economic inquiry without the constraints imposed by the neoclassical framework.

The institutionalist perspective allows the economist to consider a richer variety of human motivation at the roots of economic decisions. Human worldviews and values can become variables in the explanation of economic phenomena, rather than being excluded from the analysis by assumption, as they are in neoclassical theory. Though not all institutionalists take advantage of this aspect of the method, the Christians who write in this tradition make alternative motivations important in their theories. Thus, not all institutionalist theory qualifies for acceptance by Christians on this ground.

An institutionalism with this kind of rich account of decision-making can become a useful tool in Christian education, since it suggests that faith commitments make a difference to economic behavior, and affect the performance of the economy. This gives reason and purpose to the task of Christian education, and overcomes a fatal defect of neoclassicism.

Institutionalism admits a wider range of empirical evidence than the neoclassical school. Much attention is given to introspective accounts by decision-makers, the evolution of economic institutions through historical time, and qualitative data. These are mostly neglected by the neoclassicals in favor of quantitative variables.

Institutionalists are not enamored of mathematics, and tend to be quite indifferent about whether their theories can be couched in mathematical form. This removes a significant self-imposed constraint of the neoclassicals.

DIRECTIONS FOR THE FUTURE

The Christianity and economics literature of the past fifteen years has built a firm base for future work by scholars of all persuasions. There are a number of directions this work can take.

Amending Neoclassicism

Scholars who see some hope for amending the direction of neoclassical economics may follow the suggestion of Richardson [1988] and continue to work at the frontiers of neoclassical theory, taking advantage of the flexibility it offers to reinterpret the mathematical models in a way more consistent with Christian values. Such work may move in directions that secular scholars are unlikely to take.

Answering the Methodological Critique

The responses that have been offered so far to the methodological critique have generally been unsatisfactory. Though the philosophy of science is unlikely to offer much help in its present state, contemporary accounts, such as the sociology of knowledge school, may provide suggestive insights.

Developing the Austrian Alternative

The Christian writers who have opted for the Austrian approach have so far failed to connect their work very firmly with the basic biblical principles or with the dual critique. The economic analysis they have offered has been of the most abstract kind, and often is naive in its handling of historical and statistical data. A Christian version of Austrianism, distinct from extant versions, may be needed.

Developing a Critique of Institutionalism

Thus far, no serious critique of institutionalism has been offered by Christians. Those who wish to opt for a neoclassical or Austrian approach must develop such a critique if they wish to persuade the growing number of Christian institutionalists.

Developing Institutionalism

A Christian version of institutionalist economics needs to be clearly articulated at the level of theory content, and must be distinguished from the variety of secular institutionalist models that are extant. Christians should be doing applied work within this tradition, especially work that bears on university-level business management education. So far, much of this work has been journalistic comment on public policy matters. While such comment is important, business education in the Christian colleges is suffering for lack of relevant theoretical support, and offers a more realistic opportunity to influence the direction of our society. Professional business education is also an area where a Christian institutionalist economics can make a distinctive contribution.

Exploring the Welfare State

Many discussions of the proper economic role of the state are either based on secular values and analysis (like some of the pieces on poverty policy in Chewning [1989a and b]), or have a distressingly ad hoc tone (like Beversluis [1982], Mason and Schaefer [1990], or Tiemstra [1990, ch. 12]). Yet many of the "capitalism vs. socialism" aspects of this literature seem to come down to the question of the extent to which the state should use taxes and transfer payments to establish a social minimum standard of living. Which Christian values does a welfare state serve, and which does it subvert? Can social welfare programs be designed to accomplish their objectives with a minimum of damage? Do the experiences of western Europe and Canada have anything to teach us about the uses of the welfare state? These lines of inquiry might help to narrow the gap between the evangelical left and right on economic issues.

BIBLIOGRAPHY

Antonides, Harry. 1978. *Multinationals and the Peaceable Kingdom.* Toronto: Clarke Irwin.

Barnett, Jake. 1987. *Wealth and Wisdom: A Biblical Perspective on Possessions.* Colorado Springs: Navpress.

Beals, Art, and Larry Libby. 1985. *Beyond Hunger: A Biblical Mandate for Social Responsibility.* Portland, OR: Multnomah.

Beckmann, David. 1981. *Where Faith and Economics Meet.* Minneapolis: Augsburg.

Beisner, E. Calvin. 1988. *Prosperity and Poverty: The Compassionate Use of Resources.* Westchester, IL: Crossway.

Beisner, E. Calvin. 1990. *Prospects for Growth: A Biblical View of Population, Resources and the Future.* Westchester, IL: Crossway.

Benne, Robert. 1981. *The Ethic of Democratic Capitalism.* Philadelphia: Fortress.

Beversluis, Eric H. 1982. "A Critique of Ronald Nash on Economic Justice and the State." *Christian Scholar's Review* 11, no. 4, 330–46.

Blaug, Mark. 1980. *The Methodology of Economics.* Cambridge: Cambridge University Press.

Block, Walter, Geoffrey Brennan, and Kenneth Elzinga, eds. 1985. *Morality of the Market: Religious and Economic Perspectives.* Vancouver: Fraser Institute.

Block, Walter, and Irving Hexham, eds. 1986. *Religion, Economics, and Social Thought.* Vancouver: Fraser Institute.

Boersema, John. 1983. "A Judeo-Christian Defense of Free Enterprise-The Christian Alternative?" *Reformed Perspective* (February) 24–27.

Boersema, John. 1986. "Is Capitalism Christian?" *Reformed Perspective* (Sept.) 12–14, (Oct.) 11–13.

Boland, Lawrence A. 1982. *The Foundations of Economic Method.* London: George Allen & Unwin.

Byron, William, ed. 1982. *The Causes of World Hunger.* New York: Paulist.

Caldwell, Bruce. 1982. *Beyond Positivism: Economic Methodology in the Twentieth Century.* London: George Allen & Unwin.

Catherwood, Fred. 1983. *On the Job: The Christum 9 to 5.* Grand Rapids: Zondervan.

Chewning, Richard. 1989a. *Biblical Principles and Business: The Foundations.* Christians in the Marketplace 1. Colorado Springs: Navpress.

Chewning, Richard. 1989b. *Biblical Principles and Economics: The Foundations.* Christians in the Marketplace 2. Colorado Springs: Navpress.

PART 1: Christian Theology and Economic Methodology

Clouse, Robert, ed. 1984. *Wealth and Poverty: Four Christian Views*. Downers Grove, IL: InterVarsity.

Copeland, Warren R. 1988. *Economic Justice: The Social Ethics of U.S. Economic Policy*. Nashville: Abingdon.

Cort, John C. 1988. *Christian Socialism: An Informal History*. Maryknoll: Orbis.

Cramp, A. B. 1975. *Notes Towards a Christian Critique of Secular Economic Theory*. Toronto: Institute for Christian Studies.

Cramp, A. B. 1983. *Economics in Christian Perspective: A Sketch Map*. Toronto: Institute for Christian Studies.

Daly, Herman E., and John B. Cobb, Jr. 1989. *For the Common Good*. Boston: Beacon.

Diehl, William E. 1984. "The Guided Market System." In Clouse 1984, 85–109.

Duchrow, Ulrich. 1987. *Global Economy: A Confessional Issue for the Churches?* Geneva: WCe.

Dykema, Eugene R. 1989. "Wealth and Well-being: The Bishops and Their Critics." In Strain 1989, 48–60.

Elliott, Charles. 1987. *Comfortable Compassion? Poverty, Power, and the Church*. New York: Paulist.

Ellul, Jacques. 1984. *Money and Power*. Downers Grove: InterVarsity.

Elzinga, Kenneth G. 1981. A Christian View of the Economic Order. *Reformed Journal* 31 (Oct.) 13–16.

Etzioni, Amitai. 1988. *The Moral Dimension: Toward a New Economics*. New York: Free Press.

Gay, Craig M. 1991. *With Liberty and Justice for Whom? The Recent Evangelical Debate over Capitalism*. Grand Rapids: Eerdmans.

Gish, Art. 1984. "Decentralist Economics." In Clouse 1984, 131–59.

Goudzwaard, Bob. 1975. *Aid for the Overdeveloped West*. Toronto: Wedge.

Goudzwaard, Bob. 1979. *Capitalism and Progress*. Grand Rapids: Eerdmans.

Goudzwaard, Bob. 1986. Christian Social Thought in the Dutch Neo-Calvinist Tradition. In Block et al. 1986, 251–65.

Goulet, Denis. 1982. "Goals in Conflict: Corporate Success and Global Justice?" In Williams and Houck 1982, 219–47.

Griffiths, Brian. 1984. *The Creation of Wealth: A Christian's Case for Capitalism*. Downers Grove, IL: InterVarsity.

Haan, Roelf. 1971. *An Inquiry into the Monetary Aspects of a Link Between Special Drawing Rights and Development Finance*. Leiden: H. E. Stenfert Kroeze.

Haan, Roelf. 1988. "The Economics of Honour: Biblical Reflections on Money and Property." Geneva: WCC.

Halteman, James. 1988. *Market Capitalism and Christianity*. Grand Rapids: Baker.

Harrod, Roy. 1938. "Scope and Method of Economics." *Economic Journal*.

Hay, Donald. 1989. *Economics Today: A Christian Critique*. Leicester, UK: InterVarsity.

Heyne, Paul. 1990. "Christianity and the Economic Order." *Bulletin of the Association of Christian Economists* (Spring) 5–6.

Hill, Peter J. 1987. "An Analysis of the Market Economy: Strengths, Weaknesses, and Future." *Transformation* 4 (Summer/Fall) 40–47.

Hirsch, Fred. 1978. *Social Limits to Growth*. Cambridge: Harvard University Press.

Hoksbergen, Roland. 1982. "The Morality of Economic Growth." *Reformed Journal* 32 (Dec.) 10–12.

Jegen, Mary Evelyn, and Bruno Manno, eds. 1978. *The Earth is the Lord's: Essays on Stewardship*. New York: Paulist.

Jegen, Mary Evelyn, and Charles K. Wilber, eds. 1979. *Growth with Equity: Strategies for Meeting Human Needs*. New York: Paulist.

Kirk, Andrew. 1983. *Good News of the Kingdom Coming*. Downers Grove: InterVarsity.

Klay, Robin K. 1986. *Counting the Cost: The Economics of Christian Stewardship*. Grand Rapids: Eerdmans.

Krieder, Carl. 1987. *The Rich and the Poor: A Christian Perspective on Global Economics*. Scottdale, PA: Herald.

Lee, Robert. 1981. *Faith and the Prospects of Economic Collapse*. Atlanta: John Knox.

Linsell, Harold. 1982. *Free Enterprise: A Judeo-Christian Defence*. Wheaton: Tyndale.

Little, I. M. D. 1962. *A Critique of Welfare Economics*. 2nd ed. London: Oxford University Press.

Lutz, Charles P., ed. 1987. *God, Goods, and the Common Good*. Minneapolis: Augsburg.

Mason, John D., and Kurt E. Schaefer. 1990. "The Bible, the State, and the Economy: A Framework for Analysis." *Christian Scholar's Review* 20 (Sept.) 45–64.

McCloskey, Donald. 1985. *The Rhetoric of Economics*. Madison: U. of Wisconsin Press.

McCullum, Hugh, Karmel McCullum, and John Olthius. 1977. *Moratorium: Justice, Energy, the North, and the Native Peoples*. Toronto: Anglican Book Centre.

McKee, Arnold. 1987. *Economics and the Christian Mind*. New York: Vantage.

Meeks, M. Douglas. 1989. *God the Economist*. Minneapolis: Fortress.

Mieth, Dietmar, and Jacques Pohier, eds. 1980. *Christian Ethics and Economic: The North-South Conflict*. New York: Seabury.

Mirowski, Philip. 1989. *Against Mechanism: Saving Economics from Science*. London: George Allen and Unwin.

Mishan, Ezra. 1967. *The Costs of Economic Growth*. London: Staples.

Monsma, George N. 1980. "The Socio-Economic-Political Order and Our Lifestyles." In Sider 1980a.

Monsma, Stephen V., ed. 1986. *Responsible Technology*. Grand Rapids: Eerdmans.

Mott, Stephen Charles. 1987. "The Bible and Economics: What Does It Tell Us?" *Transformation* 4 (Summer/Fall) 24–33.

Mullin, Redmond. 1984. *The Wealth of Christians*. Maryknoll: Orbis.

Nash, Ronald H. 1986. *Poverty and Wealth: The Christian Debate over Capitalism*. Westchester, IL: Crossway.

Nash, Ronald H. 1989. "The Subjective Theory of Economic Value." In Chewning 1989b, 80–96.

National Conference of Catholic Bishops. 1986. *Economic Justice for All: Pastoral Letter on Catholic Social Thought and the U.S. Economy*. Washington: U.S. Catholic Conference.

Niebuhr, H. Richard. 1951. *Christ and Culture*. New York: Harper & Row.

North, Gary. 1973. *An Introduction to Christian Economics*. Nutley, NJ: Craig.

Novak, Michael. 1982. *The Spirit of Democratic Capitalism*. New York: Simon & Schuster.

Olasky, Marvin, H. Schlossberg, P. Berthoud, and C. Pinnock. 1989. *Freedom, Justice, and Hope: Toward a Strategy for the Poor and Oppressed*. Westchester, IL: Crossway.

Owensby, Walter L. 1988. *Economics for Prophets*. Grand Rapids: Eerdmans.

Pemberton, Prentiss, and Daniel R. Finn. 1985. *Toward a Christian Economic Ethic: Stewardship and Social Power*. Minneapolis: Winston.

Plantinga, Alvin C. 1990. *The Twin Pillars of Christian Scholarship*. The Stob Lectures. Grand Rapids: Calvin College.

Preston, Ronald H. 1986. The Legacy of the Christian Socialist Movement in England. In Block 1986, 181–201.

Rasmussen, Larry. 1981. *Economic Anxiety and the Christian Faith.* Minneapolis: Augsburg.

Richardson, J. David. 1981. "Christian Doubts about Economic Dogmas." In *Christianity Challenges the University*, edited by Peter Wilkes. Downers Grove, IL: InterVarsity.

Richardson, J. David. 1988. "Frontiers in Economics and Christian Scholarship." *Christian Scholar's Review* 17 (June) 381–400.

Schaeffer, Franky, ed. 1985. *Is Capitalism Christian?* Westchester, IL: Good News.

Shinn, Roger L. 1985. From Theology to Social Decisions and Return. In Block 1985, pp. 175–95.

Sider, Ronald J., ed. 1980a. *Living More Simply: Biblical Principles and Practical Models.* Downers Grove: InterVarsity.

Sider, Ronald J. 1980b. *Cry Justice: The Bible on Hunger and Poverty.* New York: Paulist.

Sider, Ronald J. 1990. *Rich Christians in an Age of Hunger.* 3rd ed. Dallas: Word. (Previous editions 1977 and 1984, by InterVarsity.)

Simon, Arthur. 1984. *Bread for the World.* 2nd ed. Grand Rapids: Eerdmans.

Smedes, Lewis B. 1965. Persons and Property. *Reformed Journal* 25 (April).

Speiser, Stuart M. 1989. *Ethical Economics and the Faith Community.* Bloomington, IN: Meyer Stone.

Stivers, Robert. 1976. *The Sustainable Society and Economic Growth.* Philadelphia: Westminster.

Stivers, Robert, ed. 1989. *Reformed Faith and Economics.* Lanham, MD: University Press of America.

Storkey, Alan. 1979. A *Christian Social Perspective.* Leicester: InterVarsity.

Storkey, Alan. 1986. *Transforming Economics.* London: SPCK

Strain, Charles R., ed. 1989. *Prophetic Visions and Economic Realities.* Grand Rapids: Eerdmans.

Taylor, Richard K 1973. *Economics and the Gospel.* Philadelphia: United Church Press.

Tiemstra, John P. 1979. "A Tale of Two Editions." *Fides et Historia* (Fall).

Tiemstra, John P. 1988. "Stories Economists Tell." *Reformed Journal* 38 (Feb.) 11–13.

Tiemstra, John P., W. Fred Graham, George N. Monsma, Carl J. Sinke, and Alan Storkey. 1990. *Reforming Economics: Calvinist Studies on Methods and Institutions.* Lewiston, NY: Edwin Mellen.

Van Dahm, Thomas. 1983. "The Christian Far Right and the Economic Role of the State." *Christian Scholar's Review* 12, 1, 17–36.

Van Leeuwen, Mary S. 1982. *The Sorcerer's Apprentice.* Downers Grove, IL: InterVarsity

Vandezande, Gerald. 1984. *Christians in the Crisis.* Toronto: Anglican Book Centre.

Vickers, Douglas. 1976. *Economics and Man: Prelude* to *a Christian Critique.* Nutley, NJ: Craig.

Vickers, Douglas. 1982. A *Christian Approach* to *Economics and the Cultural Condition.* Smithtown, NY: Exposition.

Vickers, Douglas. 1985. *Money, Banking, and the Macroeconomy.* Englewood Cliffs: Prentice-Hall.

Waterman, Anthony. 1985. "Religious Belief and Political Bias." In Block 1985, 3–20.

Wauzzinski, Robert. 1989. "The Gospel, Business, and the State." In Chewning 1989a, 203–22.

Wilber, Charles K., and Roland Hoksbergen. 1986. "Ethical Values and Economic Theory: A Survey." *Religious Studies Review* (Summer) 208–14.

Wilber, Charles K., and Kenneth P. Jameson. 1982. "Goals of a Christian Economy and the Future of the Corporation." In Williams and Houck 1982, 203–17.

Wilber, Charles K., and Kenneth P. Jameson. 1983. *An Inquiry into the Poverty of Economics.* Notre Dame: Notre Dame University Press.

Wilber, Charles K., and Kenneth P. Jameson. 1990. *Beyond Reaganomics: A Further Inquiry into the Poverty of Economics.* Notre Dame: Notre Dame University Press.

Wilkinson, Loren, ed. 1980. *Earthkeeping: Christian Stewardship of Natural Resources.* Grand Rapids: Eerdmans.

Williams, Oliver, and John Houck, eds. 1982. *The Judeo-Christian Vision and the Modern Corporation.* Notre Dame: Notre Dame University Press.

Wogaman, J. Philip. 1977. *The Great Economic Debate: An Ethical Analysis.* Philadelphia: Westminster.

Wogaman, Philip. 1986. *Economics and Ethics: A Christian Inquiry.* Philadelphia: Fortress.

Wolterstorff, Nicholas. 1983. *Until Justice and Peace Embrace.* Grand Rapids: Eerdmans.

Wolterstorft Nicholas. 1984. *Reason within the Bounds of Religion.* 2nd edition. Grand Rapids: Eerdmans.

Wolterstorff, Nicholas. 1987. "The Bible and Economics: The Hermeneutical Issues." *Transformation.* 4 (Summer/Fall).

Yoder, John H. 1986. "Minority Themes." In Block and Hexham 1986, 281–301.

3

Doing Economics, But Differently

I THINK THAT CHRISTIAN economists should do economics. That may seem too simple or obvious, but I think it is neither. Many Christian economists feel obliged to do things that are not economics. Others think that doing economics means conforming to the mainstream research paradigm. I don't think either of these approaches is adequate.

I don't think it is adequate to say that Christian economists as Christians should only address Christians. We may get a receptive hearing within the community of believers, but the temptation will be for us to preach, and most of us are better economists than preachers. It is certainly true that the secular world does not think that Christianity (or any other religion) has anything to say about the ordinary business of life, and would prefer to keep it that way. This makes it difficult for anyone bringing a religious perspective to economics to get a hearing in secular circles. Nevertheless we must persist, because the secular world is wrong. Christ is lord over all of life, not because the secular world elected him, but because he conquered death on the cross. The demands of God that we conform to God's will for our economic life come to all people. Nobody is exempted from God's call simply because they don't believe. As members of God's kingdom, it is our duty to get God's message out to the world in whatever way we can. And it is possible. There is enough of a residuum of Christianity in our culture and enough disenchantment with cynical secularism that some people are still interested in Christian perspectives on economic life.

I also don't think it is adequate for Christian economists to practice economics as usual within the mainstream neoclassical paradigm, tacking on some Christian values at the stage of policy prescriptions, after all the damage has already been done. I subscribe to what I have elsewhere called the dual critique of neoclassical economics (Tiemstra 1993). The ethical critique suggests that the neoclassical conception of what is normal and what is good in an economy is not consistent with Christian social ethics, and that the behavior assumed of economic actors is not the sort of life that Christians are called to live. Christians, it is claimed, are not utilitarians in social ethics, and their behavior should not be governed by self-interested gain-seeking. The methodological critique claims that neoclassical theory falls into ethical, conceptual, and empirical problems because the criteria used to validate it are inadequate. The positivist foundations of neoclassical theory cause economists to oversimplify human decision-making processes and to miss their meaning. (See Tiemstra et al. 1990 or Hay 1989.) The neoclassical framework thus excludes many questions that are of great importance to Christians, questions about how people's values and religious commitments influence their economic behavior, and how in turn that affects the institutional structure and performance of the economy. If it is true (as Catholic commentator Michael Novak 1982 claims) that market economies only work properly when embedded in a democratic political system and a Christian culture, we need to have theories to explore how those connections work. If we Christian college faculty members are trying to teach our students that their Christianity should make a difference to their behavior in the business world, we need theories to tell us how and why. If God says that following God's commands will cause us to prosper, we need theories that give us ways of exploring that relationship. Neoclassical economics doesn't do it, so we need different approaches.

When you leave the neoclassical mainstream it is likely to be said by some of the more narrow-minded members of the profession that you are not doing economics. To illustrate, let me relate an anecdote from my long-departed youth. During my undergraduate days some of my friends thought they could end the Vietnam War by persuading everyone who was against the War to not buy Coca-Cola or Wonder Bread anymore. I had a hunch that this would not work, but I thought it was worth exploring why someone might think it would. I proposed this as a dissertation topic at MIT. I had a lot of trouble finding faculty who were willing to serve on my committee. Even some people I considered comparatively broad-minded told me they would not help because this topic was not economics. Why was it not economics? Because it was not a question that could be comfortably addressed within the neoclassical framework. I am forever grateful to Charles Kindleberger, who understood that this was indeed an economic question, and who drove me to think the problem through thoroughly and explain it clearly (Tiemstra 1975). To all of you I say: Do economics, but do not let your idea of what is economics be defined by conventional theories.

If one accepts the dual critique and rejects mainstream economics, there are then a couple of options. One is to start from first principles and build a brand-new, specifically Christian economics from the ground up. (This is the approach advocated by my colleague Roland Hoksbergen, 1994.) Post-modernist methodological theory almost suggests that this is the proper course. If any and every scientific theory or interpretive effort reflects the historical and social circumstances and the religious presuppositions of its author, then the only way to make sure that your own commitments are the ones reflected in the theory is to concoct the theory yourself. And why not? There are an infinity of possible theories that are at least broadly consistent with the data, and no foundational criteria for choosing among them. Economists are a very conservative bunch, and won't give up neoclassicism easily, but there is really no reason for us to continue to cling to a theory we are uncomfortable with.

I don't think this is good strategy, not because I disagree with post-modernist methodology (I don't), but because it gets economists away from doing economics, and for that reason it doesn't work. (In the late 1970's and early 1980's at Calvin we did a lot of sitting around, figuratively looking out the windows, trying to think up a whole new Christian economics. Maybe if we had had real windows then it might have worked better.) When economists sit around trying to think up a Christian economic paradigm, they start doing philosophy and theology instead of economics. While I admire versatility in scholars, most of us went into economics because that is where our comparative advantage lay. Besides, science almost never progresses this way. Because we are so caught up in the axiomatic method and in the history of our own discipline, we forget that science almost always progresses when somebody comes up with a novel solution to a difficult question. This suggests that we should be looking at difficult questions.

The problem with the axiomatic method is that it teaches us to focus on dreaming up lists of axioms and proving theorems. The object of the game (and for many people it is just a game) is to see how many theorems you can prove from a short list of assumptions. This may be a good way to get published, but it is a bad way to make progress in economics, especially if you are trying to be self-consciously Christian in your approach. It is much more important to be able to tell a good story about what is going on. And by a "good story" I do not mean one that is simply entertaining and has lots of funny made-up words to stand for abstractions that only an economist would find useful. By a "good story" I mean a plausible account of the causes and effects of certain economic actions, an account that would have meaning to an educated layperson because it would connect to everyday experience. (I count watching CNBC as an everyday experience.) This is not only a good way to invent new theories, but it is also a good way to teach the old ones and to test their truth.

As I said, we should be taking on difficult questions because that is the way we make progress. It is important to take these questions in manageable pieces. Reading somebody like Novak may give us a taste for grand theories and big questions, but we are much more likely to be successful if we take on a narrow part or a particular instance of a problem or question rather than a great abstraction. Some particular feature of the narrower problem may suggest an approach that turns out to have much wider application than first appears. For example, I think the reason we have made so little progress toward a convincing account of the proper economic role of government is that we insist on thinking of the problem in exactly those grand abstract terms. I think we do better when we start by thinking about particular instances of government intervention in the economy, like welfare programs, or health care, or environmental regulation. When we have analyzed enough of those particular cases we may have a basis for a general theory.

But even when setting out with the task of developing a plausible story about a relatively narrow or particular problem, we still have to have some broader theoretical framework which can connect the problem to an overall vision of the economy and suggest the outlines that a solution may take. If we reject the neoclassical framework because of the dual critique, what alternative is there for us? Different Christian economists make different choices. Some Third-World Christians have chosen Marxism, but to most of us that seems like a poor choice. Some have chosen Austrianism, but those of us who accept the dual critique believe that most of it applies to Austrianism just as well as it does to neoclassicism. The best choice for many of us seems to be post-Keynesian/institutionalist economics, which

I will call PKI for short. (Here I am following the practice of Wilber and Jameson 1990.)

PKI economics is appealing to many Christian economists because it does not suffer from the problems pointed to in the dual critique. Let me put that in a more positive way. PKI approaches allow us to introduce Christian values into our concept of what is normal and right about an economy without always tripping over the Pareto-optimality concept. It does not insist that the most important value an economy could serve is to respect people's preferences, or maximize liberty in making economic choices. It allows us instead to focus on full employment, the condition of the poor, the decentralization of economic power, the care that is taken with the natural environment, and the quality of the relationships between buyer and seller. PKI economics also permits us to ask all of those especially important questions about how people's values and religious commitments affect their economic behavior, and the influence that has on the structure and performance of the economy. As a Christian I believe that these things are vital tasks for my professional life. Neoclassical economics does not allow me to do them, and PKI economics does. In the wonderful appendix to *Habits of the Heart*, Bellah and colleagues express it this way:

> Social science as public philosophy, by breaking through the iron curtain between the social sciences and the humanities, becomes a form of social self-understanding or self-interpretation. It brings the traditions, ideals, and aspirations of society into juxtaposition with its present reality. It holds up a mirror to society. By probing the past as well as the present, by looking at "values" as well as "facts," such a social science is able to make connections that are not obvious and to ask difficult questions. In this book, for example, we have tried to disclose the nature of American individualism, its historical and philosophical roots as well as its present reality, and we have asked whether individualism, as the dominant ideology of American life, is not undermining the conditions of its existence. That question is simultaneously philosophical and sociological, and an answer to it requires not just an evaluation of arguments and evidence but ethical reflection (1985, pp. 301–2).

There are some problems with PKI economics. The main trouble is that it is not just one thing. Unlike other schools of economic thought, PKI theory can be very different depending on who is doing it and what problem they are addressing. This can be frustrating if you are looking for a starting point in approaching some new problem. It also means that not all institutionalist thought turns out to be equally useful for the purposes of making a Christian economics. Many institutionalists are so preoccupied with the role of social conventions and the role of power in their analysis that they maintain the neoclassical assumption of self-interested, gain-seeking economic actors. (Dugger 1984. See my comments in Tiemstra 1992.) Some are just as preoccupied with the goal of economic growth as the neoclassicals are. Some don't think that full employment is very important. (Galbraith 1973, pp. 250–53. See my comments in Tiemstra 1979.) Therefore Christians must be careful in deciding which among all the PKI theories that are available are useful for our purposes. It also must be said that some areas of PKI economics are simply underdeveloped, but that can probably be said about any school of economics.

Is there any use at all for all that neoclassical stuff we all took such time and trouble to learn? Any use, that is, besides teaching it to our students and developing the dual critique? Yes, I think so. Neoclassical economics is a very powerful tool for examining the pecuniary incentives that people face, and the fact is that pecuniary considerations matter to people, some more than others. The problem is the assumption that pecuniary considerations are all that ever matter, an assumption that the late Donald MacKay would have called "nothing-buttery" (1974). The problem with MacKay's approach is that he would continue to do his research as if the mind were nothing but a biochemical organ, even as he acknowledged that it was not so. He depended on his idea that brain science and other accounts of mind were complementary theories to enable him to pursue these as separate agendas. I don't think that will work for us as economists because I see PKI and neoclassical theories as competing and mutually inconsistent rather than complementary. While appropriating some neoclassical tools for particular purposes, we must continue to reject the neoclassical story. Even in analyzing financial markets, where it would seem that pecuniary motives are dominant, the neoclassical story has trouble accounting for expectations formation, waves of euphoria and pessimism, changing attitudes towards risk, the effect of financial innovation on corporate governance, and motivations behind individual saving and investment behavior.

In what sense is what I have described a distinctively Christian economics? PKI economics as done by Christians does not take sentences from the Bible and try to incorporate them whole into an economic theory. In that way it is unlike what "creation science" tries to do in natural science, or even what "Christian reconstructionist" economics has tried to do in our field. The economics I have described would not be rejected out of hand by secular economists because of overtly theological content. Which is to say it is economics, not theology or philosophy or ideology. But neither does it proceed on the basis that theological presuppositions are entirely irrelevant to the enterprise of economic analysis. It is economics that is informed by Christian theology and ethics. The questions are formulated with their importance for Christian social ethics in mind. The view of human beings as moral agents and essentially religious beings at its foundation is based on a Christian philosophical anthropology. The evidence considered includes not only overt behavior, but also the reasons people give for behaving as they do. The theoretical framework is chosen because of its openness to these considerations.

It should be clear by now that I am not trying to "baptize" a particular school of economic thought, claiming that it is the only option for Christians. I have chosen it for reasons that I take to be related to my faith, and I will try to persuade you to do the same. But I recognize that Christians have and will continue to hold a number of different positions on this issue. I agree with my colleague Kurt Schaefer (1992, p. 134) and I have said before in print (1989), nothing that depends on some particular economic theory should ever be given confessional status. Though I sometimes wish that the church paid as much attention to us as it does to the geologists and astronomers, I devoutly hope that nothing ever happens in our field to resemble the war waged on some of our Christian colleagues in the natural sciences by the advocates of "creation science."

Neither will I be accused of "immanentizing the eschaton" (Gay 1991, pp. 207–14; 1992, pp. 358–61). It is always tempting to claim that your intellectual opponents have become secularized while only you maintain the true faith. It is a temptation that we have to resist. The irony of the situation is that those who are the targets of these accusations are usually those scholars who are most concerned about the integration of faith and learning and most active in pushing forward a Christian intellectual agenda. In other words, they are the ones least likely to be secularized. To spell out the obvious, most of us hold many beliefs at the same time, but not all of those beliefs have the same status. The beliefs that I express on Sunday when we all say the Nicene Creed I hold at an entirely different level than the beliefs I have published on the reasons for economic regulation or the non-existence of an equality/efficiency tradeoff. The beliefs expressed in the Creed I hold with a much higher degree of conviction, and they are not the sort of beliefs one would abandon in the face of contrary evidence. They are also more basic beliefs, in that they have implications that reach to all areas of life, which is not the case with beliefs about economic propositions. It is simply a matter of good intellectual hygiene to try to achieve some consistency in one's beliefs at these different levels. I respect all those who make that effort, even if they disagree with me on issues like the validity of the dual critique.

The alternative is to compartmentalize our lives so that Christianity is our faith in church on Sunday but irrelevant to the lives we lead the rest of the week. That is a half-hearted Christianity that is not fully responsive to the claims of Jesus Christ on our lives, and it does not save us from secularization. It also makes the enterprise of Christian higher education pointless. In his excellent new book, Stephen Carter (1993) recognizes the danger that Christians will try to enlist their faith in support of some predetermined ideological or political position, and in the process cheapen or secularize that faith (Chapter 4). But there is another danger that he fears far more-the danger that religion and religious rhetoric will be banished from all discussion of public affairs because of some mistaken epistemology or some misguided definition of the separation of church and state. A fear of immanentization that would cause us to bracket off our Christianity from our public life would just as surely lead to the secularization of the public square. As Carter says, we must not be afraid to confront differences in policy views among Christians, but we must not let our views be dismissed from the discussion just because they come justified with religious rhetoric. Carter puts it much better: "Because of this ability of the religions to fire the human imagination, and often the conscience, even of nonbelievers—as, for instance, the civil rights movement did—the religions should not be forced to disguise or remake themselves before they can legitimately be involved in secular political argument" (p. 232).

Christian economists should do economics, and what's more, they will do economics. Should they do distinctively Christian economics? As Alvin Plantinga says, the case that they should is simplicity itself: "As Christians we need and want answers to the sorts of questions that arise in the theoretical and interpretative disciplines; in an enormous number of such cases, what we know as Christians is crucially relevant to coming to a proper understanding; therefore we Christians should pursue these disciplines from a specifically Christian perspective" (1990, p. 40).

REFERENCES

Bellah, Robert N., et al. (1985), *Habits of the Heart*, New York: Harper & Row.

Carter, Stephen L. (1993), *The Culture of Disbelief*, New York: Basic.

Dugger, William M. (1984), *An Alternative to Economic Retrenchment*, New York: Petrocelli.

Galbraith, John K. (1973), *Economics and the Public Purpose*, New York: New American Library.

Gay, Craig M. (1991), *With Liberty and Justice for Whom?*, Grand Rapids: Eerdmans.

———. (1992), "When Evangelicals Take Capitalism Seriously," *Christian Scholar's Review* 21, 343–61.

Hay, Donald A. (1989), *Economics Today: A Christian Critique*, Grand Rapids: Eerdmans.

Hoksbergen, Roland (1994), "Is There a Christian Economics?," *Christian Scholar's Review*.

MacKay, Donald M. (1974), *The Clockwork Image*, Downers Grove, IL: InterVarsity.

Novak, Michael (1982), *The Spirit of Democratic Capitalism*, New York: Simon & Schuster.

Plantinga, Alvin C. (1990), *The Twin Pillars of Christian Scholarship*, The Stob Lectures, Grand Rapids: Calvin College.

Schaefer, Kurt C. (1992), "Creation, Fall, and What?," *Faculty Dialogue* 18, 125–34.

Tiemstra, John P. (1975), *Protest Through Market Action*, unpublished dissertation, Massachusetts Institute of Technology.

———. (1979), "The Affluent Society Revisited," *Anakainosis* (Fall).

———. (1989), Review of Ulrich Duchrow, Global Economy: A Confessional Issue for the Churches?, *Calvin Theological Journal* 24, 326–27.

———. (1992), "Varieties of Institutional Economics: The Theory of the Firm," *Forum for Social Economics* 21, 43–50.

———. (1993), "Christianity and Economics: A Review of the Recent Literature," *Christian Scholar's Review* 22, 227–47.

Tiemstra, John P., et al. (1990), *Reforming Economics*, Lewiston, NY: Edwin Mellen.

Wilber, Charles K., and Kenneth P. Jameson (1990), *Beyond Reaganomics*, Notre Dame, IN: Notre Dame University Press.

4

Why Economists Disagree

ECONOMISTS TEND TO GET somewhat defensive about the disagreements within the profession. There have been so many bad jokes about economists' disagreements that there is a tendency to protest (almost too much) that we don't really have that many disagreements. We claim that the disagreements people observe concern policy issues, about which disagreement is legitimate, and not analytical issues, where we have established what the scientific truth is, at least to the level permitted by the current state of research technology and information.

Our students and other laypeople do not believe this, and by saying it we undermine our own credibility. Anybody who has ever watched the journalist Jim Lehrer try to moderate a debate between two economists knows perfectly well that economists disagree vehemently, not just about policy preferences, but even about analytical issues and about their accounts of past events in the economy. Restoring our credibility with the public means that we economists have to get clear about the nature of our disagreements.

This paper seeks to prove four statements: (1) Economists disagree about theories, not just policies. (2) These theoretical disagreements are based in part, but not entirely, on disagreements concerning methodological issues. (3) These disagreements are based mostly on disagreements concerning normative issues, i.e., how economies should function. (4) Normative issues can be discussed rationally, and economists should make use of such discussions in teaching their discipline. The paper concludes with a discussion of the disagreements among evangelical Christian economists.

ECONOMISTS DISAGREE ABOUT THEORIES

In their very well-known and popular textbook, the distinguished economists William Baumol and Alan Blinder describe the role of economic theory in policy debates as follows: "While economic science can contribute the best theoretical and factual knowledge there is on a particular issue, the final decision on policy questions often rests either on information that is not currently available or on tastes and ethical opinions about which people differ (the things we call 'value judgements'), or on both." (Baumol and Blinder 1997, p. 17)

Some economists emphasize our lack of information as the source of disagreements. Milton Friedman in his famous methodology piece says, "I venture the judgment, however, the currently in the Western world, and especially in the United States, differences about economic policy among disinterested citizens derive predominantly from different prediction about the economic consequences of taking action—differences that in principle can be eliminated by the progress of positive economics—rather than from fundamental differences in basic values, differences about which men can ultimately only fight." (1953, p. 5) Similarly, James Tobin, asked by Arjo Klamer how Keynesians and new classicals move the discussion forward, replies: "Well, in the end we have to look for models that explain what goes on and fit the data. I realize that this is very difficult. But economics is difficult." (Klamer 1983, p. 111)

Lester Thurow believes that differences in the valuation of economic outcomes is at the basis of most economists' disagreements: "Liberal and conservative economists most frequently disagree on who ought to be hurt and who ought to be helped. Their technical disagreements on who will be hurt and who will be helped are much less frequent." (1982, p. 177) Curiously, Thurow and Friedman use the same example, minimum wages. Friedman believes that more data will resolve differences in economists' predictions about the effects of minimum wages, and the disagreement will disappear. Thurow sees no disagreement over the predictions, the issue between the "Theory X" and "Theory Y" advocates having been resolved by the data. (1982, p. 178) Rather, he sees a disagreement over whether low income people should have more income. Part of this difference can be attributed to the time when they were writing. In fact, Thurow may find more disagreement about the minimum wage now in the wake of the work of Card and Krueger. But there is some serious confusion here, brought about by a refusal to admit the possibility that the disagreement is over theory.

Most of the debates going on now concern issues where we have a great deal of information, and in which there are generally agreed-on social goals. The disagreement is about economic theories ("science"), and that is why the debate is so sharp and acrimonious. Debates about theories tend to have a "right versus wrong" or "enlightened versus stupid" tone because most people still live with the idea that theories are value-free and can be validated scientifically, without reference to any tastes and ethical opinions about which people differ. Value judgments are at the bottom of many theoretical disputes, but we have to be clear that the argument is about theories, not social goals.

For example, consider the debate over health care reform. Both sides of the debate claimed to be seeking exactly the same goals: reduction in the rate of increase of health care costs, and universal access to the health care system. For a few weeks, the debate seemed to be about whether "universal access" meant 92 percent or 97 percent of the population covered by health insurance, but most folks quickly realized that difference was not important. When it comes to health care systems, lack of information as to the ramifications of various policies is not a problem. Among the OECD member countries there exists just about every option for health care reform that could possibly be considered, and for twenty years economists have been avidly pursuing grants to travel abroad and study them. We should be able to predict what policies and institutions will achieve our goals, if economics is a "science."

So what is this debate about? Economic theory. Would the cost levels in the system be checked more effectively with a system of government-sponsored buyers' cartels or without them? Does universal coverage require a mandate, or can it be achieved by structuring tax incentives differently? Answers to these questions depend on how one understands the behavior of economic agents in the context of different institutional structures. The social goals are identical, and the empirical evidence we have can be interpreted in such a way as to be consistent with either point of view. If the debate were about goals, it would be easy to politely agree to disagree. But when the debate is about theories, it looks like the other side is just plain wrong. That's when the heavy rhetorical artillery is brought out, and things get ugly.

Or consider tax reform. The Treasury Department and the Congressional Budget Office say that if we replace the Federal income tax with a flat tax on consumption, and if income levels don't change, lower- and middle-income people will pay more tax, and the affluent will pay less. Those who favor this change claim that the economic growth stimulated by reform will more than make up for the additional tax middle-income people would have to pay. On net, everybody will be better off. Those who oppose the reform suggest that the additional economic growth will not be enough to compensate middle-income people for the tax increase. Both sides share the same goals: economic growth first and foremost, and after that, more or less proportional taxation. The evidence from the tax reform experiments of the 1980's is used by both sides to support their case. The 1980's can be seen as either a golden age of inflation-free growth stimulated by two rounds of tax reform, or it can be seen as a time of increased poverty and inequality brought about by the same reforms. Evidence from other countries is used in similar ways by both sides. Both views accurately account for the facts, and the values at the bottom of each interpretation are clear enough. The differences concern the understanding of human behavior in an economic setting, or in other words, economic theory.

I have deliberately chosen examples that are somewhat distant from the traditional debate over rules versus discretion in macroeconomic stabilization policy, to reinforce the point that this problem is central to the core of economics. The macro policy question is pretty obviously a case where everybody shares the same goals, reducing both inflation and unemployment, and stabilizing the path of GDP, and where everyone is working from the same data. For a long time economists misclassified this disagreement, because without satisfactory micro foundations, macro theory was not included in the core of high economics. The rules/discretion argument could then be considered a mere policy dispute, not a theoretical dispute, so it could be dismissed as reflecting mere preferences. The more work is done on micro foundations, especially by the so-called new Keynesians, the clearer it becomes that this really is a theoretical dispute.

THEORETICAL DISAGREEMENTS ARE BASED IN PART ON METHODOLOGICAL DISAGREEMENTS

The tendency for economists of different schools to disagree about methodology is not exactly news. We have known since the 1970s at the latest that Milton Friedman is a methodological instrumentalist, and Paul Samuelson is a conventionalist. Thus methodology must play some role in the rules/discretion debate, and probably plays a part in the larger argument between the Chicago School and New England-style economics.

More generally, there is a strong and widely noticed correlation between the modernist methodological position and economic orthodoxy, while heterodox economists tend to dissent from the modernist methodology. D. N. McCloskey has thoroughly documented the uses (and abuses) of modernism in the defense of orthodox economics, on the way to her critique of that methodology (1994). Stanley Wong has explicated a postmodern or antimodern methodological basis for Cambridge School, Post-Keynesian economics (1973), and William Dugger has done the same for contemporary institutionalism (1979).

The difficulty comes in explaining the exceptions. McCloskey is the best case in point. To the endless frustration of the heterodox economists who admire and use her work on methodology, McCloskey remains a Chicago school economist and a political libertarian, albeit of the "good old Chicago School" and not the contemporary variant. She writes, "Rhetorical alertness can be used to force the dominant groups to face up to institutionalism or Marxism or feminism or Austrianism, as they should. But nothing inside the rhetoric itself implies one or the other view. . . .Rhetorical self-awareness is consistent with the genuinely neoclassical. Rhetoric is consistent with any number of beliefs about the economy, between which one can toggle." (1994, pp. 394–95) McCloskey is capable of having a serious conversation with Arjo Klamer on common methodological ground, and the result is a pleasure to read—clear and educational and entertaining (McCloskey 1994, ch. 24).

The next question to ask then is whether it is possible for an economist of modernist methodological persuasion to be heterodox in his theoretical beliefs. McCloskey suggests the difficulty of this when she suggests that the mainstream has used modernism as a wall to keep alternative views out of the discipline, or at least out of most conversations about economics. But some of the most brilliant and clever heterodox economists have managed to get a hearing from the mainstream by adopting the forms (and possibly some of the substance) of modernist, "scientific" economic rhetoric, complete with the heavy-duty mathematics. McCloskey brings up the names of John Roemer and Jon Elster (1994, p. 353). I think of the work of Thomas Weisskopf, Samuel Bowles, and David Gordon (1983).

It is not that hard to come up with a modernist critique of mainstream, neoclassical economics. No scientific theory is immune from all criticism concerning its logic or how well it fits the evidence. It is pretty easy for dissenters in economics to find cases where the mainstream does not deliver on its promise to explain all economic behavior (in the Chicago version, all behavior period), or to predict future economic events well. Constructing a modernist case for a heterodox theory takes more effort, because usually we first have to argue that the scope of the evidence admitted into the conversation must be broadened. There is no reason in official modernism not to accept questionnaire data, historical accounts, qualitative evidence, introspection, and so on. Many other social sciences routinely admit such data. But because mainstream economics is so eager to emulate classical physics, the scope of the permissible evidence has been narrowed unnecessarily and excessively. There is a large premium on mathematical cleverness in economics, perhaps especially for those outside the mainstream.

So in spite of the noticeable correlation between methodological views and theoretical views, methodology is not the root of all economic disagreements. It is possible to be an antimodernist neoclassical, and to be a modernist dissenter. There are such people around.

THEORETICAL DISAGREEMENTS ARE MOSTLY BASED ON NORMATIVE ISSUES

People are undoubtedly attracted to theories that help justify policies that their instincts say are right, but economists do learn from their theories. More important, economic theory is inescapably normative, and people's views about how an economy should work come in clusters that are logically related. As Hausman and McPherson put it, "One cannot assess explanations in economics without making moral and prudential judgments about how acceptable it is to act for particular reasons." (1996, p. 49) The values and worldviews that imply certain policy conclusions also form the foundations of the economic analyses that justify those conclusions.

Take the Chicago School "economic" theory of regulation as an example. The foundation of this theory is the proposition that people always act in their own selfish material interest. Belief in this proposition can help to justify the view that government should be restrained as much as possible, since officials can never act in the public interest. That certainly coincides with the deep-seated ideological views of most Chicago economists. But the restraint-of-government conclusion is not the only possible conclusion that can be drawn from such analysis. In fact, it has often been noticed that George Stigler and other founders of this line of theory draw heavily on the work of Marxist economists and historians like Gabriel Kolko. These scholars are also inclined to think that government processes are vulnerable to capture by narrow private interests, but by bringing in different auxilliary values and hypotheses, reach very different conclusions about the proper role of government.

Furthermore, economists have learned a great deal from the construction of the "economic" theories of regulation. It has helped to persuade policy-makers, industrialists, and other economists (even those with different ideological preferences) that the deregulation of some industries, among them long-distance phone service and the airlines, would be a good idea. The Chicago economists themselves have learned some things about which industries are more likely to be regulated, and which are the most promising targets for reform. But the "economic" theory poses a major methodological difficulty for those who accept it. It suggests that people accept theories based on their own selfish, narrow, material interests, and that therefore economic analysis is not meant to be enlightening, but only to justify preconceived ideas. The Chicago economists reject this implication of their theory, but it puts them in a position of being inconsistent.

So these conservative, or perhaps more accurately, libertarian economists believe not only that people invariably behave in a self-interested, hedonistic way, but that this is normal ("rational") and right. Morally, people are entirely and only responsible for their own wellbeing. A person is wrong to expect that others will be or ought to be looking out for his or her welfare, and is simply mistaken to think he or she has such an obligation toward anyone else. The individual person is the fundamental unit of society, and so individual liberty for all is the most important value to uphold. A society makes progress through individual achievement in overcoming scarcity. Competition restrains private power, but government use of force is dangerous and unchecked. To prevent tyranny and oppression, strong constitutional rules restraining government power are required. Such a society will be dynamic and prosperous.

In contrast, liberal or interventionist economists believe that people sometimes behave in a self-interested, hedonistic way, especially when only material values are at stake. But people are concerned about other things as well: stability, security, sustainability, family, and a degree of material equality. They act on these values in their economic lives, but more especially in their political involvements and decisions, and the success of a society is to be measured by how well all of them are achieved. This is normal and right, because morally people are responsible for each other: "Love your neighbor as you love yourself." Human life is given meaning in commitment and service to others. A society progresses as people make and fulfill these commitments, and all of these values are realized. Government is a social tool to be used pragmatically toward the end of achieving social and economic progress. Government's tendencies towards oppression are checked by political competition in a democracy, but private economic power needs to be restrained by social mores or by laws. These beliefs lead to the development of public interest and institutionalist theories of regulation. From these theories we learn how to make regulation more efficient and effective, and we get an idea how policy-makers assess the relative importance of various natural monopoly, externality, distributional, and economic development issues. Just as libertarians are inconsistent in believing that people abandon self-interest in their academic pursuits, interventionists are somewhat inconsistent in believing that people abandon self-interest in their political pursuits, while believing it largely determines their economic behavior. (Some institutionalists have tried to escape this bind. See Tiemstra 1992.)

These two theories are mutually incompatible, and each side has been known to accuse the other of being foolish or wrong, particularly in the context of political campaigns. Traditional positivist philosophy of science would suggest that somebody will eventually devise a crucial experiment that will finally result in the rejection of one of the theories in favor of the other. This is unlikely. The reason it is unlikely is not because it is hard to do experiments in economics, or because we only get one run of history. If anything, economists have too much data, and it is too easy and cheap to run mindless regression equations. The reason it will not happen is because the differences between the two theories are based on differences in worldviews and values, not on gaps in our knowledge or incorrect reasoning by one side or the other. Even though they help determine what theories we believe, worldviews and values cannot be refuted by crucial experiments. They speak to the interpretation of the evidence, and there are an infinite number of interpretations that can be given to any single set of facts. If different definitions of the facts are permitted (pace Jim Lehrer, who tries to rule them out), the number of possible interpretations is a higher order infinity. Each side is right, given its worldview, and it is a mistake, as well as being bad manners, for one side to accuse the other of being wrong or stupid.

NORMATIVE ISSUES CAN BE DISCUSSED RATIONALLY

If these theoretical disputes are in fact based on differences in worldviews and values, or the interpretation of the facts, are we not back in exactly the same position where the principles textbooks left us? No, for two reasons. First, the principles books deny that economists disagree about theory, and as we have seen, that is false. Not only is it false, it is not credible for our students and the general public.

Second, the principles books identify value judgments as tastes. That is, what you believe about the moral nature of human conduct is in the same category as whether you like mushrooms and onions rather than lettuce and tomato on your hamburger. It cannot be discussed; it is just a personal preference. There is no such thing as truth, there is only personal opinion: "You can't argue about politics or religion." Furthermore, it is probably not worth discussing, because in textbook economics, the analysis of efficiency really determines how everything turns out anyway, without any additional ethical premises. This is also wrong and not credible to our students.

Value judgments, ethical principles, and normative economics can be discussed. Philosophers have been doing it for centuries, and we all have learned a great deal in the process. It is possible to discuss whether a system of ethical principles is internally consistent, to discover additional implications of the system that may not have been obvious at first, and to explore the applications of the system under different difficult circumstances. We can explore how a social ethics arises out of a particular religious tradition, or out of historical experience, or out of other aspects of culture. We can examine the ethical principles that would support commonly accepted social mores. We can assess the appeal of an ethical system, based on how well its implications comport with our common-sense notions of right and wrong, or the commonly accepted rules of our society. We can also look at how these commonly accepted ideas change through time, and what historically caused those changes. All of these topics are the common substance of courses in social ethics in philosophy departments.

I would not want to suggest that principles of economics courses should be turned into courses in social ethics, but I do believe that education works better when courses in one discipline build on what students learn in others. Our students would understand our subject better if we connected it with social ethics, at least by acknowledging commonly accepted moral standards at the appropriate points in the discussion. For example, we could admit that most people believe that there is intrinsic value in work, that equality of opportunity is important, that misrepresentation of a product is lying and is wrong, that poverty is a bad thing, that certain forms of competition are not considered fair, and that opportunistic pricing is widely condemned in our society. We could point out that changes in some social mores have affected both economic analysis and public policy, for example, the changing view of the ethics of income distribution, and the growing acceptance of gambling as a legitimate form of entertainment. Above all, we need to point out the ways in which the debate over philosophical individualism affects disagreements over so many issues in economics.

Actually, there are some economic policy issues that just cannot be discussed without value premises of one kind or another being introduced, if covertly. Many textbooks pretend to offer a value-free discussion of the Social Security issue. The social-insurance aspect of this program is usually dismissed summarily as a kind of political ruse used to generate middle-class support for the program, without acknowledging that many people believe that ethics demands that beneficiaries should receive from the program only the actuarial value of their contributions, no more and no less. Textbooks invariably focus more attention on the contribution of this program to the federal fiscal deficit than on its effects on the distribution of income, an emphasis that itself reflects an ethical judgment. A better approach would be to integrate a frank discussion of the ethical issues involved in this program with the analytical discussion. Discussion of the ethical foundations of the policy differences between economists must be included. Students could use the knowledge they obtained in their philosophy and history classes, and would no longer view economists as either complete cynics, or as ideologues trying to pass off their own ethical "tastes" as scientific truth.

This kind of frankness about ethics might also change the kinds of research questions that economists ask. In many cases, actions are considered to be ethically right or wrong because of their consequences. Economists try to have fun with people by pointing out that economic policy actions often have unintended consequences, which raises questions about their ethics. Useful as this sometimes can be, another approach would be to consider whether actions considered by economists to be inefficient might have other kinds of benefits, or whether in some cases efficient policies may have detrimental side-effects on other social goals.

WHY DO CHRISTIAN ECONOMISTS DISAGREE?

Most evangelical scholars have always insisted that theories are important. How we understand the world has so much to do with how we act in everyday life, and since religion is a vital part of that life, our understanding has a lot to do with how we live out our religious commitments. Furthermore, we have claimed for a long time that religious commitments and value judgments are inextricably involved in theory choice and validation. The popular modern idea that science is value-free and therefore uncontroversial is a notion that we never accepted, and now the post-modern world is coming around to our view.

What damps this happiness is the fact that the Christian community is every bit as divided over these theoretical issues as the rest of the world is. One day Ralph Reed's Christian Coalition calls a Washington press conference to announce its legislative agenda, with the expectation that it will get the full support of the Republican majority in Congress. A couple of days later, Jim Wallis and Tony Campolo, two leaders of the evangelical left, call their own press conference to announce an opposing program. Here are two groups that both qualify for the label "evangelical," and yet they disagree as sharply as Phil Gramm and Bill Clinton. It is possible to conclude from this that the Modern position is right—religious commitments and values have nothing to do with matters of economic analysis. It's either right or wrong. But then what is the source of the disagreement? Social goals and ethics? Careful examination of the rhetoric on each side suggests that just as with the secular politicians, the goals don't differ. It is comforting that they share these goals, because people with a common religious faith ought to share some ground in the area of social ethics.

Differences among Christians are certainly nothing new. It remains a scandal, but we have grown used to it. If we can disagree among ourselves about things like infant baptism, why should it be surprising that we disagree about social and economic policy? Let us be clear about the source of the disagreement, though. If we disagree about theory rather than social goals, then let us rejoice in our common understanding of goals, and work on the theory level with grace and generosity, understanding that our theoretical disagreements are legitimate, and not necessarily the products of ignorance, stupidity, or an inappropriate faith in some secular economic ideology (Tiemstra 1993).

The sense that Christians share social and economic goals has led to some attempts to find common ground on policy. The three Oxford Conferences on Christian Faith and Economics that have been organized by Ronald Sider have tried to achieve such common ground among evangelical economists. The premise of the conferences is that differences among evangelical economists can be bridged by a common commitment to the authority of the Scripture and a common desire for careful factual analysis. Though common statements have been produced, they have been less successful at generating genuine agreement at the level of policy (Schlossberg et. al. 1994, pp. 3–30). The reason for this failure has been the conference organizers' habit of ignoring differences that exist at the level of economic theory. This is not to say that recognition of theoretical differences would lead to agreement, but that the sense of frustration and failure that surrounds the effort could mitigated if the real differences were recognized and respectfully discussed.

I think that a similar problem is at the bottom of Craig Gay's analysis of differences among evangelical economists (1991, ch. 4). Gay is critical of economists who purport to be integrating their faith with their economic analysis, on the ground that they are turning their economic beliefs into religious dogma. In fact, many of the evangelical economists Gay criticizes are trying to find an account of economic behavior and interaction that fits with their theological understanding of the human nature. In the process, some of these economists become dissenters from mainstream economics. But that dissent, however passionately it is expressed, is still essentially a matter of economic theory, and not basically about social ethics or goals. It certainly is not about the Church.

If evangelical Christians can carry on among ourselves a civil and constructive debate about social theory, bearing in mind that differences in values, commitments, and interpretations even within our own community are legitimate, we can set an example for the larger society. A lot is at stake. Political debate in our country needs less heat, and more light.

REFERENCES

Baumol, W. J., and A. S. Blinder. 1997. *Economics: Principles and Policy.* 7th ed. Fort Worth: Dryden.

Dugger, W. 1979. "Methodological Differences Between Institutional and Neoclassical Economics." *Journal of Economic Issues* 13, 899–909.

Friedman, M. 1953. *Essays in Positive Economics.* Chicago: University of Chicago Press.

Gay, C. M. 1991. *With Liberty and Justice for Whom? The Recent Evangelical Debate over Capitalism.* Grand Rapids: Eerdmans.

Hausman, D. M., and M. S. McPherson. 1996. *Economic Analysis and Moral Philosophy.* New York: Cambridge University Press.

Klamer, A. 1983. *Conversations with Economists.* Totowa, NJ: Rowman & Allenheld.

McCloskey, D. N. 1994. *Knowledge and Persuasion in Economics.* NY: Cambridge.

Schlossberg, H., V. Samuel, and R. J. Sider, eds. 1994. *Christianity and Economics in the Post-Cold War Era.* Grand Rapids: Eerdmans.

Thurow, L. 1982. "Why Do Economists Disagree?" *Dissent* 29 (Spring) 176–82.

Tiemstra, J. P. 1992. "Varieties of Institutional Economics: The Theory of the Firm." *Forum for Social Economics* 21, 43–50.

Tiemstra, J. P. 1993. "Christianity and Economics: A Review of the Recent Literature." *Christian Scholars' Review* 22 (March) 227–47.

Weisskopf, T. E., S. Bowles, and D. M. Gordon. 1983. "Hearts and Minds: A Social Model of U.S. Productivity Growth." *Brookings Papers on Economic Activity* no. 2, 381–450.

Wong, S. 1973. "The 'F-Twist' and the Methodology of Paul Samuelson." *American Economic Review* 63 (June) 312–25.

5

Notes from the Revolution
Principles of a New Economics

CHRISTIANITY AND MAINSTREAM ECONOMICS

As CHRISTIANS WE NEED to bring to our scholarship and science all that we know, both from our observation of God's handiwork in creation, and from our reading of God's written word. Our economic science must be founded on our understanding of humankind made in God's image, with awareness, reasoning, and moral consciousness. And as the three persons of the Godhead live together in society, so too human beings live in society, with and for each other. In the fall, humans have become infected by sin, and so are capable of wrong actions as well as right ones. The line between good and evil runs through the heart of all human institutions, be they churches, schools, businesses, unions, markets, political parties, or governments. All are prone to fail the moral test, as all are capable of responding to God's norms of goodness and love. So as Christians we can never fully embrace an economic science founded on individualism and hedonism, and can never accept an economic ideology based on the infallibility of some human social institution.

The heterodox approach to the integration of Christianity and economics as it developed in the 1970's and 1980's thus begins with what I have called the dual critique of neoclassical economics (Tiemstra, 1993). The ethical critique disputes the account neoclassical economists give of human nature, particularly the assertion that all relevant human motivation stems from a natural and laudable drive to maximize ones standard of living. This forecloses consideration of how human behavior responds to the Great Commandment to love God above all and ones neighbor as oneself. The implication that economic institutions and policies should be aimed at efficiency and growth is also brought into question, since it does not comport well with the Christian social ethics implied by the Great Commandment.

The methodological critique first denies that "positive" economics can be value-free, as is often claimed. Second, it questions the orthodox preoccupation with statistical evidence, to the exclusion of experimental evidence, survey evidence, and narrative history. This is partly a consequence of an unhealthy preoccupation with mathematical models to the exclusion of other forms of analysis.

Economists who accept the validity of the dual critique are faced with the problem of how to do economics outside the mainstream. Most fall in with one or another of the heterodox schools: Post-Keynesian economics, institutionalism, or the social economics tradition. A few wind up in the Austrian camp. Others are convinced of the need for a distinctively Christian economic theory, and they have produced some interesting analyses. Many of these efforts overlap, since none of these schools offer a general canonical model in the way neoclassical economics does.

THE POST-MODERN METHODOLOGICAL REVOLUTION

While post-modernism is not a new thing, it did not have much impact in our discipline until economists began to produce serious methodological works in the middle 1980's. The post-modern message confirms what both parts of the dual critique had maintained all along: contrary to the assertions of logical positivism, all theory is value-laden. It is not possible to do science without dragging into it all of your personal baggage, including not just your personal history, but also your social position, your values, and your faith. Some founders of the approach may have wanted to explode all grand controlling meta-narratives or foundational beliefs, on the ground that none can be proven valid, but that is no more possible than shedding your own skin. Christian post-modern realists were able to carve out a place for distinctively Christian scholarship (Wolterstorff, 1984; Westphal, 2000; Hoksbergen, 1994).

The implications of this are truly startling. A science founded on a Christian worldview can be just as valid as one founded on a naturalist worldview, or a Marxian worldview, or a feminist worldview, or a libertarian worldview, or whatever (on feminist economics for example, see Hewitson, 2007). Some Christian philosophers who were early proponents of this approach became highly esteemed in their profession. New societies of Christian scholars were founded in many of the academic professions in the 1980's, including of course, the Association of Christian Economists. At the same time, many new heterodox learned societies were founded, including for example the International Society for Ecological Economics, the Society for the Advancement of Socio-Economics, and the International Association for Feminist Economics. Many traditional Christian undergraduate colleges (like Wheaton and Calvin) developed a new emphasis on faculty research and scholarship, and Christian research universities (like Baylor and Notre Dame) developed new interest in the integration of faith and learning.

The post-modern move not only confirmed the idea that theory is value-laden, but it also reinforced the rest of the methodological critique. The preoccupation of economists with mathematical models and statistical tests was a byproduct of the positivist anointing of the naturalist worldview. If we did not have to accept naturalist foundations, economics did not have to model physics, so we could ask people what they were up to, and pay attention to the answers. The controlling meta-narrative of a canonical general theory is shown to be unnecessary to a scientific approach. This has helped convince us that values and religious commitments matter to economic behavior (Milberg, 2007).

A brief aside: Christian interest in the integration of faith and learning is no longer widely stigmatized in the larger academic world (though being a heterodox economist is still hard). Therefore the pressure to become more secular in a drive for academic prestige is no longer as strong as it was back in modern times. Christian college and university presidents who are terrified of their institutions' going secular can relax a little. There are more and more excellent Christian research scholars, interested in the integration of faith and learning, and hiring them will not hurt the institution's academic reputation at all. At Calvin we used to have trouble finding young economists who knew what we were talking about. Now we find quite a few who have read some good stuff about the integration of Christianity and economics as grad students, and some who are already members of ACE. On the flip side, Calvin and other Christian colleges have been raided for Christian scholars by some of the best universities in the country, though this is still not as common in economics as in some other disciplines.

THE CANONICAL MODEL HAS BEEN DISCREDITED

The greater openness to new forms of evidence, together with a growing embarrassment about the lack of sound psychological foundations for economics, has led to the gradual discrediting of the neoclassical canonical model, and its abandonment for research purposes (I'm thinking here of Samuelson's *Foundations of Economic Analysis* or Hicks's *Value and Capital*). This was helped along by the post-modern suspicion of all controlling general theories (Davis, 2006; Colander, 2000).

I think economists were first brought up short by some evidence that came in over the transom from social psychology, at the time (in the 1970's) when economists were becoming interested in establishing a tie between utility and happiness. Yes, there was the Easterlin Paradox, with the implication that people's happiness was influenced by the consumption of others (Clark, et al. 2008 reviews a lot of this literature). But beyond that, there was evidence of an adaptation-level effect, and a self-serving bias leading to upward comparisons of well-being (Scitovsky, 1976). Then too, there was all that money that businesses were spending on advertising and promotions that had no information value, and therefore (in utility theory) should have had no serious effects (Etzioni, 1988).

Behavioral economics has been around for a while. I remember one of my undergrad professors telling us that experiments showed then (back in the 1960's) that the only economically rational people were graduate students of economics. By the 1990's, the body of experimental evidence had grown enough to make a noticeable impact on the profession, and the behavioralists had added a lot of survey data that confirmed their conclusions. Daniel Kahneman's Nobel Prize helped a great deal. We now know that people don't always do what's in their economic interest, especially if it conflicts with their sense of fairness, or "common sense" ideas. People are notoriously bad at evaluating risks, and tend to be very short sighted. Economists began to pay attention to puzzling little economic anomalies that they had ignored for decades. Every principles textbook these days has a box discussing why people leave tips in restaurants when they're out of town.

Macro phenomena, especially business cycles, have always presented problems for the canonical model. In the early 1970's the failure of Keynesian stabilization policies gave greater urgency to the search for micro foundations for macro theory. The failure of the "new classical" medicine to cure the economy in the early 1980's led to greater despair. Finally we have come to realize that business cycles have not disappeared, and they simply cannot be explained in a world of rational expectations and flexible prices. This also counts against the canonical model.

The revelations of widespread corruption in the American business community that came at the turn of the century I think shocked many economists more than they let on (Healy and Palepu, 2003). The redesign of executive compensation and corporate governance that had occurred over the last thirty years was supposed to align the incentives of agents with the interests of their principals, and high levels of pay were supposed to insulate executives from temptations to be dishonest. Besides, there were the banks, the analysts, the auditors, and the SEC to protect the integrity of capital markets. But it all failed. It turned out that human perversity could wreck even supposedly self-correcting markets.

The growth of price discrimination as an acceptable business practice has also helped to undermine the neoclassical paradigm (Tiemstra, 2006). Many economists have become comfortable with price discrimination as a second-best solution to allocation problems in monopolies, especially natural monopolies. But it remains prima facie evidence that monopoly power exists in these markets. And we are talking about some of the more important, technologically progressive, growing markets, like Internet access and pharmaceuticals. The notion that all or most markets are perfectly competitive, or even workably competitive, is more and more difficult to maintain.

Then there is the issue of distribution. The mythology of economics has always been that a growing, industrialized economy will tend to become more equal over time. This is the generalization embodied in the Kuznets Curve, but apparently it goes back as far as Adam Smith (Van Til, 2007, p. 20). The canonical model is not well suited to handle the issue. But the increased inequality of incomes in our growing U.S. economy over the last thirty-five years is one of the great public concerns of our time. The reality is inconsistent with the Kuznets rule. We look for answers, but without considering the role of power in the economy, there are none.

As a result of all this, the neoclassical research program has basically been abandoned. Cutting-edge work these days is behavioral economics or specially conceived bits of game theory. Some of it is not economics but freakonomics, the application of clever econometric devices to questions that are of such narrow scope that they are not particularly interesting. OK, that's a little unfair. Sometimes the questions are interesting. But often the questions are outside the traditional subject matter of economics, and they certainly are not informed by insights from the canonical model. The theorizing is strictly small scale and ad hoc. Not that this is bad. It is possible to make progress this way, as I argued at the ACE tenth anniversary conference (Tiemstra, 1994). Research questions need to be asked about important and centrally economic issues, even if they are narrowly framed. The recent move is a big change from (as Shackle called it) "the Years of High Theory."

Research is one thing; teaching is something else. We still pay our bills by teaching the canonical model to our students, much to their frustration. Part of this is the natural conservatism of economists, or if you will, inertia. Part of it is the revenge of the teacher for having been made to jump through these hoops as a student. Part of it is our lack of imagination about how to organize an economics course around anything but the canonical model. But this is my plea for open-mindedness. We need to decide what the great ideas and great questions of our discipline are. We need to decide what we really know about the economy. Then we must organize our courses around that. The publishers will resist, but you can publish anything yourself on the Web. Go for it (Tiemstra, 1999, 2000).

Economists have not yet learned to be circumspect in basing their policy advice on the old model. Behavioral economics has made some inroads in practical finance, especially issues like the design of retirement savings programs. But many economists still base their mechanism designs on the assumption of pure economic rationality. For example, they resist the Corporate Average Fuel Economy standards, preferring increases in fuel taxes to induce consumers to buy more fuel-efficient cars, indirectly driving the automakers to provide them. Thirty years of short sighted, irrational decisions by drivers and the Detroit Three should convince us that fuel taxes alone are unlikely to work. There is still controversy over Sarbanes-Oxley and other new regulations to control abuses in financial markets. The claim is that all the wonderful information available to investors now will cause them to discipline management, and obviate the need for regulation. One would think that Enron had never happened. I could go on, but the point is made. We have to stop making policy recommendations based on a model that we all know is wrong.

PRINCIPLES OF A NEW ECONOMICS

A new economics for Christians should not be vulnerable to the dual critique, but rather should draw on the best of the new research that has taken place outside the neoclassical paradigm. First, there needs to be a fuller and more thoughtful understanding of human nature. People are inescapably religious, as John Calvin and Bob Dylan ("You've got to serve somebody.") both have noted. People work out their understanding of ultimate values and the spiritual world not just in thought and art and scholarship, but also in their daily economic behavior. This means that although behavior is certainly influenced by economic incentives, it is driven by meaning and purpose, by people's sense of what is good and right, helpful and fair. It is not always strictly self-interested, but is informed by duty, moral obligation, and by love and care for others. Much of what is done by specialists in marketing and advertising is based on appeals to these deep-seated motives.

At the same time, the human race has fallen into total depravity, and people respond to temptations as much as to values, emotions, and incentives. Our self-serving bias and distorted perceptions of our own intelligence, strength, and immunity from harm lead us into decisions that are not rational (in the fullest sense) or wise. There is no salvation apart from divine intervention in the person of Christ Jesus. Therefore, no system of rules, institutions, or policies will guarantee that individuals will always do the right thing, or that the right outcome will always be achieved. A humane economics will always seek to understand before it prescribes or instructs.

Economic efficiency and growth are not the only values people serve in their economic lives, and are not the only proper objectives of private or public economic policies (Finn, 1989). Equally important is justice and fairness, both commutative and distributive. Sustainability, both economic and ecological, is essential for the survival of the planet, and human beings with it. In more biblical terms, we call this the stewardship of God's creation, which God declared to be good, though it has become fallen at our hands. As Christians we also give much attention to the dignity and value of human individuals as bearers of the image of God, however tainted they may be by sin. This leads to a basic concern with the quality of human relationships within economic institutions. As economists, we are interested in how people organize and manage the use of resources to achieve all of these values.

The institutions of an economy give different degrees of power and discretion to people in different positions in society, even as the economy develops with the division of labor. This is liberating, because it means that people have the freedom to make real choices and achieve the ends they believe in. It also means there is scope for people to behave irresponsibly, in particular, to exploit others who have less power. Economists should be able to analyze the distribution and use of economic power.

Because we have real power and real choices, the goodness and rightness of economic outcomes cannot be guaranteed by any particular set of economic institutions, rules, or policies. Good and right choices by economic actors are also required. Economics is not about achieving a world in which outcomes reflect human desires. It is about moving toward a world in which economic outcomes reflect God's will, as much as we can discern it in our imperfect state.

THE NEOCLASSICAL COUNTERREVOLUTION

As I remarked earlier, economists tend to be a conservative bunch, and many within the profession want to save the old paradigm. Part of this is a generational thing. Many who became economists in the prior epoch are loath to see their knowledge go out of date. Many were attracted to economics by the values that inform the old paradigm, and still believe in them.

The counterrevolution begins by reasserting the fundamental assumption about human nature: people are rational, and pursue their self-interest. Apparently irrational behavior can be explained as resulting from lack of correct information, mistaken reasoning, or misplaced incentives. Such irrational behavior can lead to inefficient economic outcomes. Fortunately, it is within the ability of economists to fix these problems, when they have the opportunity to do so. Information costs can be reduced, and accuracy improved. People can be educated to calculate costs and benefits properly, and to ignore emotion and incorrect "common sense." Incentive systems can be designed so that rational, well-informed actors will always do the efficient thing, which is the right thing, and efficient outcomes can be achieved. (The methodology of this view is discussed at length in Caplin and Schotter, 2008. Fullerton and Stavins, 1998, applies it to environmental economics, and Burtless, et. al., 1998, to international trade.)

The counterrevolution also maintains that efficiency is the ultimate value, out of which all others can be bought. You can protect the environment if you want, or treat people well, or redistribute income, but you will pay a price. In principle, market values are supposed to reflect non-pecuniary preferences, but in practice most economists opt for GDP growth over all other goals. The research reflects these priorities.

The counterrevolution holds that market competition (or at least "workable" competition, or "potential" competition) is enough to keep private accumulation of power in check, and prevent exploitation from occurring. This means that for all our talk about "the science of choice," in the end economic outcomes are determinate. It is also this assumption of competition that stands behind the proposition that right incentives mean right conduct and right outcomes.

This approach uses the results of the new behavioral economics to avoid the circularity of the neoclassical system, breaking the identity of preference and choice. It also is consistent with the way most economists do analysis. However, it is very hard to reconcile with the empirical evidence, because it is trying so hard to rescue the neoclassical paradigm. In addition, it brings out the worst in economics: its paternalism, and its tendency to function like a religion itself, by claiming to save us from our sins, and create a heaven here on earth (Nelson, 1991).

THE REVOLUTION IS NOT FINISHED

The new mainstream research is attractive to heterodox economists, Christian and otherwise, who have long felt that the neoclassical approach was unsatisfactory. Economists in general no longer seem troubled by the value-laden nature of any social analysis. The profession has a new openness to different types of empirical evidence, and to methods and results from other social science disciplines. Thanks to burgeoning research in behavioral economics, many economists are no longer committed to the proposition that all human behavior is driven by the self-interested pursuit of material gain, or that all markets are at least workably competitive. (For elaboration of this perspective, see the work in Altman 2006.) All of this goes a long way towards addressing the concerns that were expressed in the dual critique.

The biggest problem that remains is the continued preoccupation with economic efficiency as the standard for what is good, right, and even normal. It is true that economic analysis enables us to make statements about the efficiency of certain outcomes or arrangements that are more specific than we could make about their distributive justice, human solidarity, or ecological sustainability. Deadweight burdens can be estimated in monetary terms. This gives economists a franchise in public policy debates. Furthermore, once multiple goals or values are admitted into the picture, the issue of tradeoffs and synergies among the goals arises, and with it additional complications. This undoubtedly accounts for the continued popularity of the efficiency standard.

But this preoccupation comes with a price. In the first place, mainstream work continues to be subject to the criticism that it is disconnected from concerns that are central to Christian social ethics. The neglect of justice, stewardship, sustainability, and respect because standard theory doesn't have way to measure or make concrete statements about them sparks conflicts between economists and theologians that lead to much misunderstanding and ill-feeling.

The focus on efficiency also distances economists from the public discussion of economic issues, and from the everyday concerns of ordinary people, including our students. Most people do not understand what economic efficiency means, or the connection between the structure of incentives and efficient outcomes. Our refusal to say much about distributional or environmental issues convinces many of our students that we are out of touch with reality and useless, if they haven't already concluded that from studying a difficult theory that even the professor thinks is wrong.

There is also a continuing reluctance to incorporate issues of power into economic analysis. This applies mostly to market power, but also to political power, and to the power of deep pockets to determine the direction of investments in new technologies, different communities, and through philanthropy to different social goals. Without concepts related to power, how can we understand price discrimination, or increased inequality of wages, or the effects of capital mobility in a globalized economy? The resurgence of game theory in the recent era gives economists some tools to deal with power issues. With the new methodological openness, we could also raid the political scientists' toolbox, since power has always figured big in their analyses. But yet economists tend to talk as if all markets are perfectly competitive, all decisions driven by profits, and all outcomes determinate.

This is obviously untrue, and the profession risks irrelevance by continuing to base its policy recommendations on these outmoded ideas.

CONCLUSION

There has been a lot of progress over the last twenty-five years in the mainstream of the economics profession, but there is still work for Christian heterodox economists to do. The decline of the canonical neoclassical model and the rise of behavioral economics and game theory have made economics more scientific, not less. How scientific we are has nothing to do with how mathematically sophisticated or general or complete our theoretical models are. It has to do with how much we know about how the real world works, and we are way ahead of where we used to be. The science of economics is also more open to the concerns of Christians than it was in the old days, and we have to take advantage of that to bring the discipline closer to those concerns.

What remains to be done is first, to transform how economics is taught at the undergraduate level. What is done now is a crime against learning, and the sooner we overhaul it the better. Economists working in teaching-oriented Christian colleges are in an excellent position to do something about this.

Second, we need to remedy our neglect of power as an important dimension to understanding how the economy works. This is an area in which heterodox economists have specialized, and the new economics can learn much from this body of work. The tools of game theory offer the possibility of bringing new rigor to this aspect of economics.

Perhaps most important, we also need to learn how to relate our new knowledge to both sophisticated policy discussions and to the everyday concerns of ordinary people. Over the last six decades or so economists have developed a lot of bad habits that we need to shed. Economists still pretend to be doing value-neutral analysis, when we all know there's no such thing. Economists pretend that the only issue is prosperity, and ignore equality, sustainability, and charity. There's no time like now to begin the process of attuning economics to the great questions that today's world raises for Christians, and for everyone.

REFERENCES

Altman, Morris, ed. 2006. *Handbook of Contemporary Behavioral Economics.* Armonk, NY: M. E. Sharpe.

Burtless, Gary, Robert Z. Lawrence, Robert E. Litan, and Robert Shapiro. 1998. *Globaphobia: Confronting Fears about Open Trade.* Washington: Brookings.

Caplin, Andrew, and Andrew Schotter, eds. 2008. *The Foundations of Positive and Normative Economics.* New York: Oxford University Press.

Clark, Andrew E., Paul Frijters, and Michael A. Shields. 2008. "Relative Income, Happiness, and Utility: An Explanation for the Easterlin Paradox and Other Puzzles." *Journal of Economic Literature* 46 (1), 95–144.

Colander, David. 2000. "The Death of Neoclassical Economics." *Journal of the History of Economic Thought* 22 (2), 127–44.

Davis, John B. 2006. "The Turn in Economics: Neoclassical Dominance to Mainstream Pluralism?" *Journal of Institutional Economics,* 2 (1), 1–20.

Etzioni, Amitai. 1988. *The Moral Dimension: Toward a New Economics.* New York: Free Press.

Finn, Daniel Rush. 1989. "Self-interest, Markets, and the Four Problems of Economic Life." *Annual of the Society of Christian Ethics,* 23–53. Reprinted in *On Moral Business,* M. L. Stackhouse, D. P. McCann, and S. J. Roels, eds., Grand Rapids: Eerdmans, 1995, 934–44.

Fullerton, Don, and Robert N. Stavins. 1998. "How Economists See the Environment." *Nature,* 395. Reprinted in *Economics of the Environment,* Robert N. Stavins, ed., New York: Norton, 2005, 1–8.

Hewitson, Gillian. 2007. "Feminist Economics as a Postmodern Moment." *Review of Social Economy* 65 (2) 187–93.

Hicks, John. 1946. *Value and Capital.* 2nd ed. Oxford: Clarendon.

Healy, Paul M., and Krishna G. Palepu. (2003). "The Fall of Enron." *Journal of Economic Perspectives* 17 (2) 3–26.

Hoksbergen, Roland. 1994. "Postmodernism and Institutionalism: Toward a Resolution of the Debate on Relativism." *Journal of Economic Issues* 28 (3) 679–713.

Milberg, William. 2007. "The Shifting and Allegorical Rhetoric of 'Neoclassical' Economics." *Review of Social Economy* 65 (2) 209–22.

Nelson, Robert H. 1991. *Reaching for Heaven on Earth: The Theological Meaning of Economics.* Savage, MD: Rowman & Littlefield.

Samuelson, Paul A. 1947. *Foundations of Economic Analysis.* Cambridge, MA: Harvard University Press.

Scitovsky, Tibor. 1976. *The Joyless Economy: An Inquiry into Human Satisfaction and Consumer Dissatisfaction.* Oxford: Oxford University Press.

Tiemstra, John P. 1993. "Christianity and Economics: A Review of the Recent Literature." *Christian Scholars' Review* 22, 227–47.

Tiemstra, John P. 1994. "Doing Economics, But Differently." *Bulletin of the Association of Christian Economists* 23, 3–8.

Tiemstra, John P. 1999. *Economics: A Developmental Approach.* Loudonville, OH: Mohican.

Tiemstra, John P. 2000. "A New Approach to the General Education Economics Course." In E. O'Boyle, ed., *Teaching the Social Economics Way of Thinking.* Lewiston, NY: Edwin Mellen.

Tiemstra, John P. 2006. "Price Discrimination and Fairness." *Perspectives: a Journal of Reformed Thought,* 21(4), 7ff.

Van Til, Kent A. 2007. *Less Than Two Dollars a Day.* Grand Rapids: Eerdmans.

Wolterstorff, Nicholas P. 1984. *Reason Within the Bounds of Religion.* 2nd ed. Grand Rapids: Eerdmans.

Westphal, Merold. 2000. "Postmodernism and the Gospel: Onto-theology, Metanarratives, and Perspectivism." *Perspectives: a Journal of Reformed Thought,* 15, 6–10.

PART 2

Government, Business, and Society

6

Spiritual Poverty, Material Wealth

THIS HAS HAPPENED TO me more than once. A Christian colleague from another discipline, a person of conservative political views, says at some point in the conversation, "You know, you Christian economists contradict yourselves. You say that money doesn't lead to happiness, in order to convince your students that they shouldn't spend their lives seeking money. But then you want to transfer money to the poor, presumably in order to make them happier. You can't have it both ways. If money doesn't lead to happiness, there is no reason to give money to the poor. And if money does cause happiness, then Christians should not be discouraged from seeking it."

Most Christian economists have not taken this objection seriously. So far, as I know, the objection has not been offered in any formal academic setting. Many of us find it difficult to see any common sense in this accusation, so we tend to write it off. But many politically conservative Christians accept this line of argument, so it is worth addressing the rather problematic reasoning and theology that inform this assertion.

THE QUESTION OF HAPPINESS

The easy and straightforward answer to my colleagues' objection is that the Bible itself takes a position akin to ours. Indeed, Jesus' sayings contain both seemingly contradictory ideas on wealth and happiness in a single sentence: "Sell everything you have and give to the poor, and you will have treasure in heaven. Then come, follow me" (Luke 18:22). Or in the Old Testament consider the paradox represented by the opening paragraphs of Deuteronomy 15: "Give generously [to the poor] and do so without a grudging heart; then because of this the Lord your God will bless you in all your work and in everything you put your hand to" (v. 10). In other words, prosperity results from treating the poor well. This contradicts what the introductory economics books all teach, that giving generously to the poor compromises the efficiency of the economy. But that is the teaching of Scripture, and I suspect that it is our economic theories that err on this point.

But apparent contradictions in Scripture should not go without explanations either. Some of that explanation has to do with the use of the idea of "happiness" as the end product of wealth. The passages quote from the Bible do not cite "happiness" as the goal of Christians or of Israelite society. Transfers of resources to the poor are not intended to make them happier. Transfers of wealth to the poor are to help them to live dignified lives within the context of their society. Poverty is about lacking resources, going hungry and homeless. But it is also about not being a full member of society: unable to bear the responsibilities of citizenship, unable to access the institutions of society, unable to provide for a family and raise children, and unable to interact with others as equals. Helping people to escape poverty is ultimately about recognizing the image of God in them, and recognizing that exaggerated inequality of resources can shut people out of normal human social interactions. For Christians, then, poverty is a relative concept. Its definition is dependent on conditions in the society under examination. An absolute definition of poverty, such as equating poverty with homelessness, as proposed by some, does not serve Christian purposes.

Nor are dangers and special temptations of the affluence connected to the "happiness" provided by economic goods. The danger is not that we will enjoy ourselves too much or have too much fun. The danger is that we become so addicted to material comforts and pleasures that wealth becomes our god, and the pursuit of wealth becomes the meaning and purpose of our lives. We can become addicted to wealth as easily as we become addicted to alcohol, tobacco, food, sex, or gambling—and with equally devastating effects. For some Christians, conquering this problem means leaving material wealth behind and living a deliberately ascetic life, perhaps within a monastic community. For all of us in the affluent

First World, it means being very careful not to overindulge our taste for the good things of creation.

One of my economics teachers once said that the great lesson of economics was that between every minimum and maximum there is an optimum. He was thinking of pollution, work, or prices, but not of wealth itself. Most economists would say that increasing material wellbeing is the point of economic activity, and they are correct if you construe them narrowly enough. In contrast, the teaching of Christianity is that you can have too little of this world's goods and that you can have too much. There may not be a unique optimum, but for each of us there is probably a range of standards of living that are not so low that we live without dignity and are cut off from the institutions of our society—and not so high that we are in danger of thinking that we somehow don't need God.

ACCOUNTING FOR BODY AND SOUL

Both of these "consistent" positions proposed by conservative colleagues rely on theological foundations that clash with traditional Protestant Christianity. The first position is that money doesn't matter, or doesn't provide happiness, and so, there is no reason to transfer income to the poor. Presumably the correct thing to do would be to say to the poor, "Go, I wish you well; keep warm and well fed." Of course, it is exactly this kind of behavior that is condemned throughout the Bible, but especially in James (2: 14–17). The idea that only the spiritual realm matters to human wellbeing and that the physical world is less real or important is not good Christian theology. The Christian position is that the physical world is the creation of God and, while tainted by the effects of the fall, is essentially good. God himself became incarnate in order to save physical human-kind. Therefore, it matters when human beings in all their physicality do not have enough access to material goods to live a dignified life in society, and it does no good, as the apostle James says, to preach to people without meeting their physical needs.

Unfortunately, this kind of pure-form spirituality is presently popular among American Christians. A local Christian Reformed congregation once put this aphorism on its message sign: "You're only poor if you want more than you have." This is a nice sentiment, especially if you want to get out of contributing to the poor, but it has nothing to do with Christianity. Christian missionary activity in the Third World has long been based on the Jamesian principle that meeting physical needs is essential to living out our faith, but I think that among the poor of our own country, we tend to offer a lot of advice and not much practical help. We tell people that if they don't want to be poor, they should stay off drugs, stay in school, get married, and not have children until they're older. Good advice, but for people who've already made these mistakes, and regret them, this is no help. They need housing, transportation, health care, day care for the kids, tuition for school, and helpful mundane things like that. When we provide that, we get the right to preach to them.

So my conservative friend comes back and says, "All right, if the physical world matters to Christians, you have no right to criticize people for pursuing wealth." Usually left implicit is the message that we also have no right to ask people to give up hard-earned wealth to help the poor, either in the form of voluntary contributions or taxes. But this position absolutizes the pursuit of wealth. If God has no right to ask disciples to subordinate love of wealth to love for God, then God is no longer the most important thing in one's life, but wealth is. There is nothing wrong with enjoying the good things of life. Even John Calvin says, "Certainly ivory and gold, and riches, are the good creatures of God, permitted, nay, destined, by divine providence for the use of man; nor was it ever forbidden to laugh, or to be full, or to add new to old and hereditary possessions, or to be delighted with music, or to drink wine" (Book III, ch. 19, §9). However, Calvin goes on to say, "Let all remember that the nourishment which God gives is for life, not luxury . . ." In short, we must be ready to use the wealth with which we are blessed for the service of God's kingdom, including aid to the poor. We are mere trustees of wealth, and God is the trustor. Therefore God has the right to determine what people are to do with "their" wealth. When the pursuit of wealth becomes so important that it obscures the suffering Jesus in the appearance of the poor, then it has become an idol. Simply put, it has taken the place of God, and our souls are in danger.

The insistence of some conservatives that Christian economists either deny any importance to physical creation or invest it with ultimate importance is a case of what the late Christian thinker Donald MacKay called "nothing-buttery." Life is either nothing but spiritual or nothing but physical. The "nothing but" positions are, of course, both wrong. Life is both-and. Church historian Martin Marty has identified this as a major theme of American culture that has its origin in the national heritage of Protestant Christianity: "In the American experience, citizens and believers have been figuratively at war with sharp dictionary definitions that pose pure form materialism against pure form spirituality" (1995, p. 239). My conservative friends have been spending too much time with their dictionaries.

WHO DESERVES WHAT?

Another part of the implicit message of this "consistent" conservative position is that there is a difference in "deservingness" between the rich and the poor. Affluent Christians are well off because they have worked hard and earned their wealth. They are beyond criticism. Furthermore, we can tell they earned it, because we live in a market economy, and the market process only rewards the deserving. The poor, on the other hand, do not deserve help because they have not earned it. We can tell they haven't earned resources because they don't have them. To start with, this view depends on the questionable assumption that the market only rewards the deserving. This is not true, and all of us can think of counter-examples. This view also doesn't get much favor with Calvin because he regularly insisted that no totally depraved human being had earned anything better than hell. Of course, as Fred Graham (1971) pointed out, the poor have not earned the wealth given to help them, but remember that neither has the giver. All resources and wealth, no matter how they come to us, are ours only by the grace of God and not our own merit. So says Calvin: "The Lord enjoins us to do good to all without exception, though the greater part, if estimated by their own merit, are most unworthy of it. But Scripture subjoins a most excellent reason, when it tells us that we are not to look to what men in themselves deserve, but to attend to the image of God, which exists in all, and to which we owe all honor and love" (Book III, ch. 7, §6).

Of course, there is room for Christians of different political persuasions to disagree about ways of aiding the poor. There is certainly legitimate and serious disagreement about the appropriate roles for churches, governments, and other institutions in providing this help. There is also some room for disagreement about what forms of help would prove most effective, although we must also be careful not to make an idol out of effectiveness. There are different ways to define effectiveness of an anti-poverty program, and not all of them are realistic or faithful to the Biblical mandate. For instance, some conservatives focus on getting poor people employed- that is their definition of success. Getting work in the marketplace is good for a lot of poor people, but it is not the answer for all of them. Some of them need to stay home and care for children. Some will not be able to escape poverty through employment, because they lack skills or access or capacity to work. To be sure, lack of effectiveness is a drawback for a particular program, but it is not a reason for Christians to abandon the poor altogether (on this question of effectiveness, see Wuthnow 1997, ch. 11). There comes a point in the process where we have to suspend our tendency to pass judgment on people different from ourselves, and let God make the judgments while we simply offer whatever assistance we can manage.

What disappoints me most about how many conservatives handle the issue of wealth and poverty is that their positions all seem to want to supply some kind of justification for Christians not to have to give up real resources to help the poor. In the face of the teaching of the Bible, Christian theology, and the church's tradition of activism, these conservatives want to deny that Christians have any obligation to provide the poor with material support. They believe that they can justify escaping this Christian obligation by denying that poverty is real, by asserting the right of Christians to retain all their wealth, by denying that the poor deserve help, or by defining poverty so narrowly that almost nobody fits the definition. This will not do. No matter political disagreements, there is no denying that Christ demands that his followers not abandon the poor. If we do, we may abound in material wealth but wither in spiritual poverty.

REFERENCES

Calvin, John. 1559 [1987]. *The Institutes of the Christian Religion.* Edited by Tony Lane and Hilary Osborne. Grand Rapids: Baker.

Graham, W. Fred. 1971. *The Constructive Revolutionary: John Calvin and His Socio-Economic Impact.* Richmond: John Knox.

Marty, Martin E. 1995. "Materialism and Spirituality in American Religion," in Robert Wuthnow, ed., *Rethinking Materialism: Perspectives on the Spiritual Dimension of Economic Behavior.* Grand Rapids: Eerdmans.

Wuthnow, Robert. 1997. *The Crisis in the Churches: Spiritual Malaise, Fiscal Woe.* New York: Oxford University Press.

7

Poverty, Government, and the Meaning of Economics

A Discussion of Wealth, Poverty, and Human Destiny, *Bandow and Schindler, editors*

INTRODUCTION

WHAT WE HAVE HERE is two books within a single pair of covers. The essayists chosen by Doug Bandow (for the purposes of this discussion I am treating only contributions of Peter J. Hill, Michael Novak, Jennifer Roback Morse, and Daniel T. Griswold, along with Bandow's own) are called "liberals" in this book, as in classical liberals who believe in free markets and limited government. His terminology is very misleading for the average reader. In common American political terms, they are "conservatives," and that is what I will call them. They all are directing their writing here at making a case that government should not be involved in policies aimed at reducing income inequality, either within the U.S. or abroad.

The essayists chosen by David L. Schindler (here I will consider D. Stephen Long, William T. Cavanaugh, and David Crawford, along with Schindler's contribution) are called "socialists." This terminology is confusing, because they are not socialists in the sense that economists normally use the term, and they mostly seem to believe in a position that in common American political terminology would be called "liberal." I will call them "Schindler's liberals." Their essays are directed at making a case that a modern democratic capitalist economic system is not neutral with respect to the moral values and goals of agents, but biases their choices in ways that privilege the pursuit of wealth over other human values that are more important to Christians.

POVERTY AND GOVERNMENT

The conservatives' argument about government and distribution is based on some very audacious claims that are not documented, and on arguments that are not carefully thought through. Schindler's liberals do not dispute any of these propositions, since their papers address different issues entirely. I will begin by reviewing three important premises of the conservatives' argument, and discuss some of their internal problems. Then I will challenge all three of these propositions. In a later section, I will deal with the issues that Schindler's liberals bring up.

The basic argument of the conservatives goes like this:

1) Poverty in the sense that Christians mean it must be defined in absolute terms. The mere existence of a certain level of inequality in a society does not necessarily mean that anyone in that society is actually poor (Hill 2, Novak 62, 74, Bandow 317, 320). A thousand years ago, pretty nearly everybody was poor (Griswold 231). The implication is that in industrialized societies today, nearly nobody is poor (Griswold 223). A situation of inequality is preferred to perfect equality if the incomes of the least well off are higher in the unequal situation (Hill 3–4, Griswold 231). Complaints about inequality are based merely on envy, which Christians should not endorse (Bandow 319, Hill 4).

2) There is a distinction between the poor who deserve help and the poor who do not deserve help (Morse 193). Children, the elderly, and people who are sick or disabled deserve help (Novak 70, Morse 180–81). People who do not work hard or who make poor life choices do not deserve help (Bandow 321). Among the undeserving poor are mothers of children, single or married, who should be supported by the children's fathers, so that the mothers can stay at home and care for the children (Novak 71, Morse 194).

None of the writers in this book discusses the working poor, so it is unclear whether the conservatives consider them deserving or not. This is a problem, because one of the big changes in the political atmosphere in the U.S. over the last 25 years is a change in attitude toward the working poor. In the early 1980's, most people did not consider them deserving, and the Reagan-era welfare reforms were designed to exclude them from the "safety net." This was based on Charles Murray's argument in *Losing Ground* that the working poor would never accept help and would not need it. Over the next two decades this argument was discredited, and the Clinton-era reforms were based on the idea that people who "work hard and play by the rules" deserve help.

To hold that working poor are undeserving, the conservatives would have to maintain that market wages and prices always reward hard work and good intentions. Hill points to evidence from controlled experiments that differences in work effort can account for as much as a ten-fold difference in earnings (4–5). He seems to draw the conclusion that many market-based earnings differences are the result of differences in work effort (5–6), which would mean the working poor don't work hard enough. Hill (10) and Bandow (319) both claim that some poverty is due to failure of government to protect individual rights, especially property rights. The victims of these failures might be deserving, even if they work. They do not give any examples, so it is hard to know exactly what they have in mind. Hill has no problem with family inheritance playing a large role in determining the distribution of opportunity and wealth (10), which is inconsistent with the idea that the market distribution should only reward individual merit.

There is some daylight between Bandow and the others on this issue. Bandow understands that earnings differences have to do with the marketability of people's output more than with effort, and he's fine with that. Let Michael Jordan and Barbra Streisand earn their millions (321). (One wonders what he thinks of truly bad singers who earn millions.) Bandow takes the libertarian position associated with Robert Nozick that such differences are just, simply because they are the outcome of uncoerced exchanges (333). But libertarians believe that no poor people should get help, and that's a position that Christians surely cannot endorse, and none of the writers here do. If uncoerced exchanges still leave some people poor, the deserving among them should be helped, but is work enough to make one deserving? Bandow doesn't say. Bandow also takes an ambivalent position about unions. He holds they are necessary to protect the rights of the poor (323, 334), but thinks they drive up prices unjustly (315).

Another interesting aspect of Bandow's article is that he keeps arguing against positions taken by John Cort and Andrew Kirk, and disapprovingly quotes their writings (310, 317, 324) . But neither is a contributor to this volume, and there is no documentation of the quotations. In fact, there is no documentation of anything in Bandow's piece.

3) Helping the poor is properly the job of churches and other organizations of the moral-cultural sector, and must never be undertaken by government. Government is too remote and bureaucratic to make proper judgments about who is deserving and who is not (Hill 8–9, Morse 188, 207). More importantly, when government becomes involved in taxes and transfers for the purpose of redistributing income, it inevitably becomes oppressive. Redistributing income leads to the kind of oppression symbolized by Hitler's Holocaust, the massacre of the kulaks by Stalin, or the killing fields of Pol Pot (Hill 7, Novak 58, Bandow 322–33). Moderate welfare states have all failed, suffering from "bloated public budgets, imploding public pension systems, bulging jail populations, counterproductive work incentives, and hobbled national economies. Individuals, families and communities were destroyed by authoritarian paternalism, with a panoply of disastrous social pathologies ensuing." (Bandow 307–8. He does allow for a "safety net," however. 317.)

On the other hand, market-oriented reforms in mainland China have placed that country on the way to democratic capitalism, a path pioneered by Taiwan and South Korea (Bandow 323, Griswold 233–34). These writers never criticize dictators who favor the church or make market-oriented reforms, no matter how many of their opponents they murder. One thinks of Franco and Pinochet.

Since I believe that all three of these premises are wrong, I will devote the major part of my space to challenging them.

1) Poverty is always defined in the context of a particular society. The best definition I know of poverty is "the lack of opportunity to fulfill God's callings." Such opportunity involves access to the goods and services necessary to maintain a dignified life in society, opportunity to develop and use one's labor and other resources to provide as much as possible for oneself, and opportunity to make one's own economic decisions (Tiemstra et al. 1990, 234–35).

Consider Griswold's thought experiment. He claims a society where everyone makes $1000 is less good than a society where half the people make $2000 and half make $20,000. In the latter, he claims, the poor have more access to necessary goods than in the former. But this is unlikely to be true. In the former society, everybody rides the bus. In the latter society, many people have private cars, and there are no busses. The fraction of the poor who can't afford a car are in trouble, especially if there are not enough of them to generate demand for jitneys or combis. They are cut off from health care, educational opportunities, church, competitive shopping, and worst of all, jobs. They need help, but of course they're not deserving. In many communities in the U.S. today, you cannot escape poverty if you don't own or can't drive a car (Fletcher et al. 2002). A similar problem occurs in the housing market. Unequal incomes drive up the relative price of housing, meaning that the lower end of the market gets housing that has "filtered down," and consequently is subdivided into very small units and is in dilapidated condition.

We know quite a bit from comparative international data about the effect that income inequality and relative poverty have on social problems such as crime, education, pollution, and health. Relative poverty drives up the cost to government and moral-cultural institutions of dealing with such social problems, and is a drag on economic growth (Tiemstra 1992). The idea that greater inequality will cause the least well off to benefit from economic growth is contradicted by the data. We know that because of increased inequality in the U.S. over the last 30 years, the average worker has not benefited from economic growth. The median real wage for non-supervisory workers is still well below its 1972 peak.

If everybody was poor in ancient times, why does the Bible go on so much about poverty? Why does the Bible insist that some people give money to other people "so that there may be equality," if all of them are poor? (2 Cor 8:13) The Bible never offers an absolute definition of poverty, nor for that matter a firm definition of a just wage or price. The Biblical record on the poverty issue makes sense only if poverty is a relative social phenomenon. All of the objections that Bandow offers to the "just wage" concept (340) apply equally to the "absolute poverty" concept.

The idea that any complaint about inequality must be based on envy is simply a case of attributing the worst possible motives to those with whom you disagree, without having any grounds for doing so. This is not an ethical way to make an argument. It is as if I were to claim that the conservatives' position is motivated only by their greed, and consequent unwillingness to part with their own money to help others. I am sure the conservatives would be offended by that.

2) Followers of God have an obligation to help all poor people without passing judgment on whether or not they are deserving. A society that meets the Biblical standards of justice will offer support to all of the poor regardless of their circumstances. This means that we will help some people who are lazy or opportunistic, but it is up to God to judge them, not us. Jesus always made clear that he helped people because of their need, and sometimes their faith, not their works. The type of help that is offered should be designed to be the most effective based on the causes of the poverty at hand.

Morse almost gets this right in her discussion of "the law of the gift" (201–5). In fact she is following Calvin and the church fathers before him in acknowledging that all of our access to wealth and material resources comes to us as a gracious gift from God, and not because of our own merit. We are merely stewards, not owners, of these resources. What Morse does not do is follow Calvin in reaching the only logical conclusion: We have no more right to the money in our pocket than the beggar on the street does. In fact, if we have two coats and he has none, he has more right to our second coat than we do (Luke 6:29). I have written on this at greater length elsewhere (Tiemstra 2002).

The idea that some limit on economic inequality is a desirable feature of a society does not stem from some idea that everyone is equally virtuous or hard working. It is based on the idea that all people bear the image of God, and that all people are loved by God. Therefore the people of God have an obligation to love all people equally and provide for them to live a life in which they can respond to God's callings to them. An excellent introduction to this line of thought is Wolterstorff 1983, ch. 4. A more modern and thorough account is Hicks 2000.

Morse offers a story from her own life as an example of what families should do to support their own (208–12). She has taken into her home and cared for a Romanian orphan boy, and her desperately ill mother-in-law. This necessitated postponing completion of her book, and fitting her publicity tour around doctors' appointments and the availability of respite care. Her only regret is that she relied too heavily on hired help. Ms. Morse's generosity and care are admirable, but since she is so immodest as to propose this as a model, let me point out the obvious. Ms. Morse's work is very remunerative, and she has an extraordinary degree of control over her own time. The choices that she has are not available to the overwhelming majority of American families. To suggest that her experience is applicable to people of average means is out of touch with reality.

A great deal of the poverty in this country results because the jobs that are available to many folks do not pay very well, even though they require very hard work. Anyone who doubts this should read works like Barbara Ehrenreich's *Nickel and Dimed*. Then compare the work effort of a front-line worker in a house-cleaning service with the workload of a corporate CEO, who is paid hundreds (not tens) of times more, and whose 60-hour "work" week includes dinner parties and golf outings. The market does not always and only reward hard work or virtue, and there is no reason to think that the distribution of market incomes has any important moral properties. The major social institutions need to do something about this. Businesses have an obligation to pay their workers fairly. Scripture is very clear about this (e.g., James 5), and so is the tradition of Christian social thought. There is no mention of the responsibilities of business to treat their workers well in this book. At the bottom of this is a faulty theory of markets, but more about that later.

3) Government is empowered to establish justice in society. Justice includes proper care for the poor and, if possible, the eradication of poverty. Government should make use of the infrastructure of the moral-cultural sector of society to accomplish these ends, but the charitable sector does not have the resources on its own to address the poverty problem adequately.

It is not clear why the volunteer deacons at First Presbyterian Church would do a better job determining who needs help than the professional social workers down the street at the county welfare office. In a lot of cases, they're the same people anyway. Though Morse dismisses this concern (188), churches can be inappropriately judgmental in their attitudes toward the poor.

The problem with Hitler's Germany and Stalin's Russia was not that the tax rates were too high. In the end, taxes and transfer payments are only money. In the larger scheme of things it is just not that important. The comparisons made by these conservative writers between democratic welfare states and oppressive dictatorships are bizarre. When it comes to oppression, I'm much less worried about high taxes than I am about an American President who seems to think he has the legal authority to incarcerate and torture anyone he wants without charges and without trial.

Access to the legal system and to the political arena in the U.S. requires substantial resources, which is why the poor often do not have adequate access, and the political system in our country represents the interests of the rich and powerful much better than those of the poor (Phillips 2002). The Biblical concern about oppression of the poor is less about legal injustice causing income poverty than about the tendency of the system to neglect the interests of those whose lack of wealth leaves them legally powerless. Bandow worries that government action will violate the commandment against theft (316), but the main worry of the reformers and the church fathers was about rich people stealing from the poor. The Heidelberg Catechism, question 110, about the eighth commandment, stresses inaccurate weights and measures, fraudulent merchandising, and excessive interest. That concern reflects the priorities of the Bible as well, as in passages like Leviticus 19, which talks about employers holding back wages, or Proverbs 16, which talks about just weights and measures in commerce.

Bandow's claim that the moderate welfare states have all failed does not stand up to the facts. The welfare states of Western Europe have lower rates of crime and incarceration than the U.S. They perform better on almost every measure of educational achievement and health than we do. They have fewer teenage pregnancies and fewer abortions. The U.S. budget deficit is a bigger proportion of GDP than that of any of the euro-zone countries. The U.N Human Development Index places the U.S. fourth in the world, behind Norway, Sweden, and Canada, and tied with Belgium and Australia (U.N. 2003, 149). We only rank that high because we are ahead of the others in per capita GDP.

THE MEANING OF ECONOMICS

Schindler's liberals devote their space in this volume to exploring the meaning of economic activity in market economies. However much business managers may want to behave in a way that reflects Christian values, the inner logic of capitalism and the environment of competition make it impossible for them to focus on anything other than economic efficiency, profitability, and the maximization of shareholder wealth. These powerful institutions, and the wealthy and powerful people who control them, transmit these values to the employees in the workplace, who have to pursue the organization's objectives in their jobs. We all then carry these values with us into our private lives, which tend to be more and more governed by a concern with wealth and economic status. These values are reinforced by the media, which are controlled by wealthy corporations, directly through ownership and indirectly through advertising, and reflect these corporate values.

The claim that these liberal writers are making is that this distortion of human values and motivations is intrinsic to the nature of capitalism. It is clear that their understanding of capitalism has been influenced by the defenses of it that are offered by the conservatives. Both sets of writers seem to accept a theory of capitalism that is based on a version of Austrian School economics, in which innovation and change drive growth, and economic development and growth are of primary importance. They believe that in a modern market economy, competitive pressures become very intense. This is especially true in the age of globalization, when markets are no longer confined to national boundaries, but the competitive process spans continents. As we all learned in introductory economics, businesses have no choice under these circumstances but to maximize profits. Any other choice leads to bankruptcy.

The conservative writers want to claim that the freedom offered by a market economy enables people to live by whatever values they choose, hopefully Christian ones. Novak says, "Empirical research seems to confirm the primacy of spirit, and to disconfirm merely materialistic accounts of human behavior." (54) He also stresses the "subjectivity of society," the ability of people to act, rather than merely behave (56–7). Novak even claims that "materialism" is on the wane, because people are buying more services rather than material goods (53). Of course, this has nothing do with the larger point about the preoccupation with wealth. Griswold claims that multinational corporations bring high environmental and labor standards with them when they invest in less-developed countries, and that as incomes grow, these countries adopt these higher standards as their own (presumably by government regulation). (225) Bandow concludes, "Liberal economics merely allows people to think of themselves in a certain way; it does not make them do so, nor would making the economy illiberal cause them to cease doing so." (327) Bandow even claims, astonishingly, that "the market rewards honesty and trustworthiness." (328) His example is the failure of the Arthur Anderson accounting firm. He does not seem to understand that this came about because of SEC regulation and enforcement of the securities laws, i.e., government action, not the market.

But when it really matters, economic development and growth trump all other values for the conservatives, so they contend that there really are no choices. Griswold fears that including provisions for higher labor and environmental standards in trade agreements will become a drag on economic growth (237), and he approves of the pressure on governments to create a "more friendly business climate" for foreign investors and local entrepreneurs alike (219). Bandow disparages "above-market wages" as "charity carried out under the guise of business" (339) He also believes that "Private monopolies usually break down quickly due to competition." (331) If the competitive process is so intense that there are really no choices, then Schindler's liberals are right, and Christian values have no place in a market economy.

My own view is that this account of how the market economy works is not useful, precisely because it places too much stress on the process of competition and the inevitability of market equilibrium outcomes. (Tiemstra 1993, 1994) That is not the way the world really is, and good thing too. Businesses and individuals do have choices to the degree that they enjoy market power, and market power is more pervasive than generally thought. Globalization tends to privilege the power of businesses over the other sectors of society, and the values of economic growth over other values, but there are ways to correct that. So Schindler's liberals are wrong that materialism and preoccupation with wealth are intrinsic to the nature of market economies. Freedom and choice are possible, and we can live as Christians in a capitalist world. Christians should be entering the business professions, in order to spread their influence, and counter materialistic values.

By failing to address the social responsibilities of business in this work, the conservatives leave the liberals' argument unanswered, and pass up the opportunity to address the deeper causes of poverty and injustice. Society has the right to expect businesses to conform to the moral norms that God requires for justice. When businesses do not live up to these responsibilities, it is no surprise that people turn to government to address problems like poverty, sustainability, and civil rights.

CONCLUSION

This book is disappointing, because it should have been better than it is. The authors represented here are distinguished scholars with long records of productive contributions to Christian social thought. But this book is inadequately researched, sloppily thought through, and carelessly edited. Instead, I recommend reading Gushee 1999 or Carlson-Thies and Skillen 1996.

More importantly, this book will confirm for many people all of their worst stereotypes of the evangelical community. Schindler's liberals seem to be only interested in airy abstractions far removed from anything practical. The conservatives come off as arrogant, self-righteous, and above all judgmental. These are the things that drive people away from the church and away from God. Our Lord Jesus was none of these things. When a common prostitute came to wash his feet, his disciples expected him to send her away. She was not deserving of their help. Jesus did not turn her away, but forgave her (Luke 7:36–50). If we want people to accept Jesus' message and join the Christian church, we need to bring our thinking and our doing closer to his model.

REFERENCES

Bandow, Doug, and David L. Schindler, eds. 2003. *Wealth, Poverty, and Human Destiny,* Wilmington, DE: ISI.

Carlson-Thies, Stanley W., and James W. Skillen, eds. 1996. *Welfare in America.* Grand Rapids: Eerdmans.

Ehrenreich, Barbara. 2001. *Nickel and Dimed.* New York: Metropolitan.

Fletcher, Cynthia Needles, Steven Garansky, and Helen H. Jensen. 2002. "Transiting from Welfare to Work," Working Paper, Joint Center for Research on Poverty, Northwestern University and University of Chicago.

Gushee, David P., ed. 1999. *Toward a Just and Caring Society.* Grand Rapids: Baker.

Murray, Charles. 1984. *Losing Ground.* New York: Basic.

Hicks, Douglas A. 2000. *Inequality and Christian Ethics.* Cambridge: Cambridge University Press.

Phillips, Kevin. 2002. *Wealth and Democracy.* New York: Broadway.

Tiemstra, John P. 2002. "Spiritual Poverty, Material Wealth, Conservative Economics. . ." *Perspectives: A Journal of Reformed Thought* (June/July) 6–9.

———. 1994. "Doing Economics, But Differently." *Bulletin of the Association of Christian Economists* (Spring) 3–8.

———. 1993. "Christianity and Economics: A Review of the Recent Literature." *Christian Scholar's Review* (March) 227–47.

———. 1992. "Equality and Efficiency: The Big Tradeoff or a Free Lunch?" *Journal of Income Distribution* (Winter) 164–82.

Tiemstra, John P., W. Fred Graham, George N. Monsma, Carl J. Sinke, and Alan Storkey. 1990. *Reforming Economics.* Lewiston NY: Edwin Mellen.

United Nations Development Programme. 2002. *Human Development Report.* New York: Oxford University Press.

Wolterstorff, Nicholas. 1983. *Until Justice and Peace Embrace.* Grand Rapids: Eerdmans.

8

Price Discrimination and Fairness

INTRODUCTION

ELDERLY PEOPLE BOARD BUSSES to Canada to buy prescription drugs for less than they are priced in the U.S. Savvy travelers use "hidden cities" and split tickets to qualify for lower airfares. Couch potatoes disconnect their TV cables every three months so they can qualify for "new subscriber" rates. Supermarket cashiers swipe their own "preferred customer" cards for consumers who "left their card at home." People think about hiring CPAs to figure out what telephone plan will be the best deal for them. Workers boycott Wal-Mart for driving down the prices their employers can charge for goods, leading to demands for wage concessions. These behaviors can be understood simply as people gaming the system for their own advantage. I think, though, that they are more usefully understood as popular resistance to pricing policies that consumers view as unfair and unjust. Economists define "price discrimination" as differences in prices charged to different customers that are not based on differences in the costs of serving those customers. (There is no particular reference to race or sex discrimination here.) As price discrimination has become an increasingly common business practice, this popular resistance has grown.

It is time for a discussion of the ethics of price discrimination. It is important to understand why businesses find this practice increasingly acceptable, while among many consumers (and voters) it continues to be perceived as unfair. As with so many issues in America today, we will find a cultural divide between those who accept price discrimination as a just and acceptable business practice, and those who do not. Though Christians can be found on both sides of this divide, it is not a matter of indifference. Price discrimination can be accepted as ethical only if efficiency is all that matters, and justice or fairness don't matter, or alternatively if we accept the libertarian idea that anything that is voluntary is *ipso facto* fair. Christians should refuse to accept either of these premises.

THE ECONOMICS OF PRICE DISCRIMINATION

The place to begin this discussion is with the economic analysis of price discrimination. For price discrimination to exist, there must be monopoly or monopsony (single buyer) power somewhere in the market. There also must be some way for the seller to differentiate customers and to prevent some of them from buying at a low price and reselling the good at a higher price.

For a long time, economists simply took price discrimination to be evidence of monopoly power, and therefore an indicator of market failure. Monopolists might use price discrimination simply to enhance their profits, or they might employ it as a barrier to the entry of new competitors into the market. Either way, it just made things worse. The only case to be made for price discrimination was the few instances where it made goods available that the market might not otherwise support. The favorite example was the small-town physician who, by charging his clients different amounts based on their incomes, could support the fixed costs of keeping his office open, and make his own income approach that of his big-city colleagues, thus justifying his quiet, semi-rural lifestyle.

This opinion changed rather radically in the 1980s, when it was demonstrated that, under certain conditions, monopoly with price discrimination produced a more economically efficient outcome than monopoly without price discrimination. At the same time, developments in public-utility regulation led to the examination of cases where price discrimination helped utilities to cover their high fixed infrastructure costs (pipes and wires) while charging low incremental-cost prices (just covering the delivered gas, water or electricity) to the most price-sensitive customers. For example, long-distance telephone callers paid very high prices that subsidized inexpensive local service, and urban phone users overpaid to support expensive rural networks. This generalized the small-town-physician case. Price discrimination became the second-best solution to the problem of monopoly power. To many economists, it became quite acceptable, especially in markets with cost structures like the utilities.' These would include the airlines, or businesses with high fixed research-and-development costs but low per-unit manufacturing costs, like software and pharmaceuticals.

PRICES, COSTS, AND FAIRNESS

Economists usually propound the principle that prices should be related to costs. Prices that reflect costs provide information to buyers about the relative scarcities of various goods and the resources that go into producing them. Buyers can then arrange their purchases to satisfy their requirements while economizing most on the things that are most scarce. Economic efficiency requires that the market price of a good be equal to the incremental cost of producing the last unit of the good. In long-run competitive market equilibrium, the price will also be equal to the average cost, the total cost divided by the total output. This assures that the profits of the industry are in line with the rate of return to capital in the economy in general, and that allocation of capital among industries is efficient. If prices are stable, or at least predictable, then buyers can plan their purchases over a period of time to be as economical as possible.

This relationship between prices and costs appeals to people because of its efficiency, but it is also perceived as fair. The situation in which equilibrium market prices are equal to costs is described as "competitive." That is to say, no agent has the power to manipulate prices so as to increase her own income at the expense of others. This is certainly no guarantee of equality or anything like it, because different parties may come to the market with different amounts of wealth or talent or access. Nevertheless, it suggests that the market itself is not rigged in favor of any particular party. That is appealing, and people generally perceive it as fair or just. Research on laypeople's perceptions of fairness indicate that while a simple markup-pricing rule is not required for fairness, price increases not related to cost increases are regarded as unfair. Unfortunately, this research has not yet extended to directly test people's perceptions of the fairness of price discrimination.

Price discrimination breaks this connection between prices and costs, in a way that is obvious for all to see. Several consequences follow. First, prices can no longer be relied on as an indicator of scarcity, and a signal to the universe of buyers about where they need to economize. Though the most price-sensitive customers may face an incremental-cost price under price discrimination, other customers will not, and may not make efficient decisions as a result. Because economizing behavior then no longer guarantees efficiency in the allocation of resources, the social utility of the price system is compromised.

Second, sellers use price discrimination to raise their profits above the competitive level. These high profits would ordinarily serve the purpose of attracting new investment into the industry, but if there are barriers to entry in the industry, new investment will not follow. Barriers to entry could include patents, high fixed costs (of infrastructure or research), regulatory restrictions, or even price discrimination itself (by leaving no group of underserved consumers). If high profits do not attract new investment and entry, then they have no social purpose, and could be perceived as simply unfair. The perceived fairness of the price system could also be undermined simply by the evidence price discrimination provides that there is monopoly power in the system, so the monopolist is able to benefit at others' expense from the structure of the market.

The use of price discrimination to support the provision of goods with high fixed costs that might not otherwise be provided by the market might be tolerated as fair in certain circumstances. The classic case of the small-town doctor derived some of its appeal from the fact that the discrimination practiced was the "size-up-the-income" variety. Poor people got a break under this practice, and the price discrimination was progressive in its distributional effect. It also counted on a general principle that people will go to the doctor when they need to, so high prices would not discourage people from seeking medical help. If higher prices for the affluent discouraged the more frugal among them from getting preventative health care, the system may not have been very efficient at all.

The modern pharmaceutical industry makes a much less appealing case for price discrimination. The way it works in this industry disadvantages those who buy their prescriptions at retail with their own after-tax dollars. In most cases, these are not the affluent, who have prescription coverage from their insurance and pre-tax accounts for the copayments, and buy at discount prices from mail-order pharmacies. The ones who pay more are elderly low- and moderate-income folks, the kind who take the busses to Canada. The industry's claims that its enhanced revenues support research and development would be more convincing if its marketing budgets were not so large, and its profits so outsized.

THE LIBERTARIAN ARGUMENT

The libertarian position holds that all trades or transactions are fair or just as long as they are voluntary on both sides, that is, as long as physical coercion was not employed to force either party into the trade. The fact that the transaction is consummated means that both parties perceive themselves to be better off having traded than they would have been without the trade. This makes the transaction just no matter how unevenly the gains from trade are split between the parties, and no matter how unequally it may treat equals.

The conservative politicians and pundits who have adopted this position as their own often refer to the justice of "capitalist acts between consenting adults in private." The point of this comparison between market transactions and sex acts usually seems designed to tweak those liberals who prefer that government regulate markets but stay out of bedrooms. It also underscores the libertarian nature of the argument. To be consistent, these conservatives would have to argue that the government should keep out of both markets and bedrooms. Most of them are not consistent libertarians. Of course, Christians do not accept the idea that mutual consent is enough to make a relationship, whether business or sexual, right or fair. Exploitation can occur even where there is mutual consent. But the libertarian approach to market fairness appeals to many business managers with responsibility for pricing decisions, and seems to have prevailed over the cost-based fairness standard in the corporate sector.

Libertarians try to justify price discrimination by pointing out the gains from trade that even disadvantaged buyers realize. The business traveler is willing to pay $1000 for an airline ticket because she is off to close a multi-million dollar deal. She can hardly complain about paying five times the price paid by the tourist in the next seat, since the trip is worth so much to her. It is not worth as much to the tourist, for whom driving is an acceptable alternative. As long as the airline has not held a gun to anyone's head, they have not done anything wrong by appropriating a larger-than-normal share of the business traveler's gain. An elderly heart patient pays $800 for a miracle statin drug because it offers a 10 percentage-point reduction in the probability of undergoing a $50,000 coronary-artery bypass operation.

Clearly the drug is worth that much to the buyer, even if it only costs about $50 to make. Some low-income customers may get it for less, but their budgets make them more likely to simply do without the drug or the operation, and so are more sensitive to price. The same goes for countries where health care is rationed, and not everyone with coronary artery disease gets bypass surgery. The libertarian argues that the customer should be grateful for the technological miracle the drug represents, even if the pharmaceutical manufacturer gets a disproportionate share of the pecuniary gain.

PERCEPTIONS, POLITICS, AND POLICY

The culture war over price discrimination has the economists, with their utilitarian perspective, lining up with the business community, who lean toward the libertarian position. Both groups tend to see price discrimination as a legitimate practice. Rank-and-file consumers are more likely to hold views in which a close relationship between prices and costs leads to a fair division of the gains from trade between buyers and sellers. There is a popular perception of price discrimination as an unfair practice, since it breaks the connection between prices and costs.

In response to this, price discrimination is being scaled back in some industries, though it rarely disappears completely. Resentment of complicated pricing schemes and resistance to high business fares have recently driven the airlines to simplify their prices and reduce pricing disparities. The airlines still cling to frequent-flyer plans, however, since they provide an entry barrier in some markets. Periodic threats by the politicians to re-regulate cable television have led to some simplification of pricing in that industry. The frustration of consumers with telephone service pricing has led to some simplification there too. Supermarket preferred-customer cards seem to have disappeared from most markets.

The pharmaceutical companies have been the most transparent in their efforts to justify price discrimination in public statements, and the most effective in their lobbying efforts to prevent any regulatory constraints on their pricing practices. So far they have blocked efforts to make re-importation legal, and to have the government regulate prices under the new Medicare drug benefit. They have also attempted to make price discrimination more palatable by providing drugs at reduced prices in poor countries, and by making a special discount card available to low-income people in this country. At the same time, they have greatly increased their marketing efforts, especially the controversial practice of brand-name product advertising in the mass media, traditionally seen as an enhancement of market power. he struggle over industry practices looks likely to continue.

The monopsony power of national chain stores like A&P, Woolworth's, and Sears led to the passage of the Robinson-Patman Act in 1935, which nominally forbade manufacturers and wholesalers from offering more favorable prices to one retailer over another. Partly though the efforts of economists, that law became a dead letter by the 1960s, but the controversy has resurfaced with the emergence of Wal-Mart as the dominant firm in retailing. Reviving the antitrust approach to the Wal-Mart problem is not promising. But the forces that eventually brought down those earlier retailing giants are likely to work on Wal-Mart too, and if their working can be accelerated, some of the retailing competition might be saved. This probably means helping the spread of Wal-Mart's logistical methods more widely in the industry.

SOME ETHICAL CONCLUSIONS

The presumption of justice is that equals should be treated equally. Furthermore, commutative justice would suggest that the appropriate reward for a seller of goods is the recovery of the costs incurred to provide it, including the opportunity cost of the seller's time and investment in the business. This way the gains from trade are appropriately distributed between buyer and seller, with neither exercising disproportionate power over the other. When prices are related to costs, it is also more likely to be the case that the allocation of resources will be efficient.

Therefore price discrimination should be presumed to be wrong, and prices should reflect production costs. In particular, it is unethical for sellers to use their market power to extract from the buyers the bulk of the value they receive from the use of the good, or for large and powerful business buyers (Wal-Mart) to be subsidized by smaller and less powerful upstream manufacturers.

What of the cases where there are high fixed costs and low incremental costs for providing a good? What do we do about the high research and development costs of drugs, the high cost of establishing a medical practice, or the high fixed cost of bringing scheduled airline service to a community? Price discrimination might be justified in such a case, as long as it can be designed to be progressive in its distributional effect.

Here is where the cleverness of economists comes in handy. Two-part prices involve a fixed periodic customer charge together with a modest charge for service. Think of your phone bill—high monthly fee, low per-minute charge. This kind of pricing is considered by some to be a form of price discrimination, but it at least has the virtue of reflecting the cost structure of the industry—in the case of phones, high cost of installing the network, and minimal incremental cost of using it to make a call. With phones, most states also have implemented "lifeline" charges, with low monthly fees and higher per-minute charges, so that customers who use the phone very little can have a lower total bill. This works with prepaid cell phones, too.

Airline price discrimination tends to be progressive as it is now, but it may become less so as businesses increasingly resist subsidizing leisure travelers. With many forms of transportation, the high fixed costs are subsidized by government, and riders are charged something close to the incremental cost of service. Busses and trains work this way for the most part. A similar model could be applied to the airlines, and has been in other countries.

Applying a model like this to the pharmaceutical business will be more difficult. Some economists have suggested that the government pay a bounty to companies that bring products to market successfully, underwriting the research and development budget. Or insurance companies and government agencies could buy access to a company's formulary by paying a lump sum up front, and then the clients could pay the unit cost of manufacturing the drugs. Though these approaches suggest greater government funding of the industry, they need not lead to government control of the research agenda, or stifle the creativity of the private drug companies.

Fairness and efficiency both demand that we find new ways to avoid price discrimination while still encouraging investment in networks and technology. Libertarian arguments that bless price discrimination do not satisfy commonly held ideas about either fairness or efficiency. Achieving a just result is not impossible, but it requires a pragmatic approach, in which government and business cooperate. This is possible when leaders in both business and government view the achievement of justice as their goal. Ideological approaches that pit business and government against one another, or that glorify self-interest, are not helpful. It is time for Christians to put forward a view of justice that has practical implications for this common business practice.

9

Financial Crisis and the Culture of Risk

BEN BERNANKE, THE CHAIRMAN of the Federal Reserve System, listed the causes of the credit boom that led to the current financial breakdown in the Josiah Stamp Memorial Lecture at the London School of Economics on January 13, 2009: "widespread declines in underwriting standards, breakdowns in lending oversight by investors and rating agencies, increased reliance on complex and opaque credit instruments that proved fragile under stress, and unusually low compensation for risk-taking."

This is not moral language, but rather the language of the scientific economist looking for explanations rather than judgments. What Bernanke described was the behavior of many important actors in the financial system. That behavior had a moral dimension, and it can only be described as irresponsible at best. Sir Josiah recognized as much in his 1938 book *Christianity and Economics*, when he talked about "the reign of law, decency, honour, industry and thrift in which alone a complex industrial system can work."(p. 189). Justified as passing judgment is, however, to understand the roots of our financial crisis we must examine how risk changed from being a morally fraught but unavoidable problem of human existence to being a commodity traded on markets like wheat or copper. The neglect of the moral reality of risk is a recent phenomenon that lies at the bottom of our problems.

The Christian church and the western cultural heritage traditionally considered risk to be a problem that was a consequence of sin in the world.

In a sinful world, things can go wrong, and often do go wrong, but the Christian trusts that God will make sure that everything works out for good. The Christian would not take unnecessary risks, because that would be to tempt God. The Christian would not try to lay risk off onto other people, because that would be to shirk moral responsibility for ones own decisions, and cause problems for others for whom we are supposed to show love. The biblical prohibition of usury can be understood in this light: borrowing at fixed interest lays the borrower's risk of failure off on the lender. Better to form partnerships where all parties share in decision-making and risk. Christians long viewed insurance with suspicion, especially life insurance, and instead formed "burial societies" in which church members for a small subscription would share the burden of funeral costs. Widows would be supported by church benevolence funds. Christians especially opposed gambling in all its forms as the unnecessary taking of risks, with no possible benefits for family or community, and in most Christian countries gambling was forbidden or strictly regulated. Though the usury prohibition was not observed after the Reformation, many of these attitudes and practices survived well into the twentieth century, and were reinforced for many by the experience of the Depression.

Practices in the world of banking and finance also reflected this cautious attitude towards risk. Most lending was done through the banking system (rather than through investment banks or the bond market), and bankers practiced "relationship banking." They took a lot of trouble to know who their borrowers were, and do a lot of business with regular customers over a long period of time, so that they understood the business, and the character and practices of the managers, very well. Regulatory limits on branching in the U.S. meant that banking was always a local affair. Bankers stayed away from making loans in industries they did not understand, even if they were the fashionable, new, high-tech, "hot" areas of the economy.

In the 1950s and 1960s all of this began to change. The development of Las Vegas as a successful resort city based on a combination of casino gambling and glamorous entertainment led cities and states all over the U.S. to rethink their opposition to recreational gambling. Virtually all the states began to allow limited casino development, and Native American tribes looked to casinos as an important source of revenue. State governments found a new source of revenue in state-sponsored lotteries, supported by heavy advertising. Compulsive gambling was treated as a problem limited to a few people, in the same category as alcoholism, and not a reason to prohibit gambling. Gambling became just another form of entertainment, with no particular moral baggage.

At the same time economists were developing the modern theory of finance. One major result of this research was the finding that the riskiness of a portfolio of loans or securities could be reduced (to a point) by diversification, and this finding gave a real boost to the mutual fund industry. The stock market did very well in this period as more ordinary people put part of their savings into stocks, confident that the mutual fund portfolios they held had diversified away any systematic risk. As economists began to understand risk better, they developed mathematical models that allowed the calculation of an "efficient" or "rational" price for risky assets of all descriptions, as long as the probability distribution of possible outcomes was known. Since risk could be priced rationally, it could be packaged, marketed, and sold in an infinite variety of forms, especially after the coming of cheap computers made complex calculations easy. People were seduced into assuming things about risky assets that they didn't really know. Even if they knew nothing about the borrower or the market, they bought financial instruments in the confidence that the assets had been priced appropriately by a competent computer program.

With the coming of the Reagan administration, there also developed a popular ideology that idealized the risk-taking entrepreneur. This way of thinking suggested that the main source of economic growth and new jobs was the taking of risks by small entrepreneurs creating new businesses, based on new technology, or at least new insight into the wants of consumers. Big corporations could also create new jobs to the extent that they could cultivate this entrepreneurial spirit, or at least imitate the more successful new businesses. Therefore to encourage growth, the returns to risk-taking had to be increased, preferably by reducing the taxation of income from capital to zero. Reagan sharply reduced income tax rates for high-income people, and reduced capital gains taxes. This period also saw the introduction of the "Roth Individual Retirement Account" and the Section 529 education savings account, both of which exempted dividends, interest, and capital gains from any taxation. President George W. Bush took this further, exempting most stock dividends from taxation and sharply reducing the estate (inheritance) tax. Of course, this ideology stands the Christian tradition on its head. Where the usury principle favored income from work and was suspicious of income from capital, the new ideology favored capital income and tried to shift the bulk of the tax burden onto wages and salaries.

The policy environment produced by the new ideology increased the degree of inequality in the income distribution. As high-net-worth families saw their standard of living increase, middle- and lower-income families saw their living standards fail to keep up with what they were assured was a growing economy. To make up for this shortfall, many families reduced their saving, and made greater use of debt that was made available to them with very few questions asked. This pile-up of household debt reduced the stability of the system in the face of a shock to asset prices, especially the prices of households' biggest assets, their homes.

The new theory of efficient capital markets and the new ideology of job creation led American and other developed-country policy-makers to advocate an integrated global capital market. This was part of what came to be called the "Washington Consensus" on globalization. By allocating capital to the most promising opportunities for job-creation and growth around the world, and by further diversifying risk, such a market would lead to global growth, the reduction of poverty in the global South, and generous profits for the providers of capital in the global North. It was only required that all countries should adopt institutions and business practices modeled after those in the successful developed countries, most notably the United States, so that the new global market would have a "level playing field."

The new technology for marketing risk led to a separation between the underwriting and pricing of risk, and the actual assumption of risk by the lender. This was the major problem with the "subprime" and "Alt-A" mortgages, but was a problem with other kinds of loans as well. Lenders relied on loan originators, servicers, and packagers to assess the risk, service the loans, put together a diversified package of risky assets and price it appropriately. For this, the servicer receives a fee. The risk is borne by the lender, who has done no investigation or "due diligence," and does not really understand the risk. This kind of behavior by lenders is imprudent at best, but the gambling culture that has grown in our society leads lenders to view this as a game, not a serious enterprise. The new tax structure encourages it. The investment banks and mortgage companies that underwrite and price these financial instruments, and the agencies that rate them, presumably have some interest in protecting their reputations, but since they bear little risk themselves, there is an overwhelming temptation to make as many loans as possible and sell them on as quickly as possible, with little attention to controlling risk. This is also imprudent and irresponsible, but nevertheless was a very profitable business until the most recent financial collapse.

The collapse brought to the surface the systemic risk inherent in these practices. Once an unexpectedly large number of loans begin to default, it becomes obvious that many of these loans are riskier than they appeared, and may not be priced appropriately because optimistic assumptions were made about the distribution of outcomes. Calculations of the efficient prices tend to be based on the assumption that financial crises almost never happen, even though we have now had four such crises in the last 25 years. With a crisis, uncertainty enters the picture. Uncertainty is different from risk. Uncertainty is the situation where the parties to the contract do not know the probability distribution of the outcomes. Under uncertainty, an efficient price for the loan cannot be determined. Investors hate uncertainty, and flee it at any opportunity. Once investors believe that they cannot know the risk involved in any loan, or determine its appropriate price, they refuse to make loans or buy risky financial assets at all. This leads to a collapse in the prices of risky financial instruments, and lending activity freezes up. The consequence for the real economy is that purchases by businesses and consumers cannot be financed, and so economic activity collapses.

Fundamentally this is a moral issue. I don't mean this only to say that clearly dishonest and fraudulent activity took place, though it surely did. Bernard Madoff and people like him took advantage of this atmosphere of optimism and trust to cheat people out of billions of dollars. Mortgage originators conspired with clients to falsify loan applications, and connived with appraisers to inflate house values. Ratings agencies paid too much attention to the wishes of their clients, and too little attention to their public duties. Investment banks and other businesses hid liabilities in off-balance-sheet entities to conceal from the investing public the degree of leverage they had taken on. Hedge funds refused to reveal anything about their investment strategies on the grounds that they were private entities open only to the super-rich, but then marketed themselves to the public through "funds of funds." There must and will be legal consequences for those involved in these activities, and new regulations designed to reduce the amount of risk in the system.

But besides this straightforwardly illegal activity, there was a lack of the kind of prudent attention that is called for by the biblical idea of stewardship. The managers of financial institutions, investment advisors, and ordinary individuals failed to take the most basic steps. Questions about borrowers and risk were not asked. Ratings were taken at face value, so independent risk assessment was not done. Investment banks, insurance companies, and hedge funds ran up too much leverage, and households borrowed too much money. A premium was placed on innovation, so new, risky derivative instruments were invented that had no real business purpose. Brokers were so concerned about selling products that they forgot about their fiduciary duties to their clients.

As we have seen, taking risks with our money, which is really God's money, is not generally a good thing to do, whether it involves borrowing for a risky venture, investing in risky financial assets, or buying too little (or too much) insurance. It calls into question our willingness to be responsible for our own behavior, our concern about the welfare of others, and our faith in God's providence. It is acceptable to take risks if it is likely that the community as a whole will benefit, so taking good business risks is acceptable. Since the Reformation, Christians have accepted that lending money at interest is a business practice that can be useful and beneficial to all people. But there must be prudence. There must be due diligence. Lending money is not a game we play for thrills, nor is it simply an easy way to make money without working; it is a serious expression of our responsibility before God. Our problem is that we have not taken it seriously enough.

The church needs to reassert moral leadership on the topic of risk. We need to stop caving in to the prevailing cultural pressures, and assert what the Bible, our moral tradition, and our experience teach us to be true. First, we must begin to preach against gambling again, not only describing it as sin but explaining to people why it is inconsistent with God's will. We also need to bring back the moral tradition that excessive debt is not a healthy thing for households or for businesses. Yes, there are good reasons to take on a prudent amount of debt to buy a house or expand a business, but debt is not a game, and it is not right to take on debt just to look for a tax break or to fend off a corporate takeover. Nor should we be financing everyday expenditures by borrowing.

The church needs to emphasize that in lending or investing, there needs to be prudence, due diligence, and a full regard for the effect of our actions on the larger community. It is not just bad business to take on risks that we don't understand. It is immoral. It puts our whole economy at risk for our lack of prudence. In our age of instant information about everything on the Internet, there is also no excuse for not investigating where our money is going. If the person soliciting your money can't answer all your questions, don't invest with them.

The church also has a witness in the area of public policy. We need to point out the dangers inherent in financial globalization. Crises spread easily from one country to another in a world of closely linked markets. Investing at a distance makes it harder to do due diligence, and makes investors more inclined to judge projects by quick summary measures, like profits, and not look into the effects on communities. We Americans also end up imposing our business practices on people whose cultures, religions, and values we don't always understand very well. This creates resentment of our power.

There are also dangers in public policies that increase income inequality and disadvantage work. Let income from work and income from capital be taxed at the same rates. This is just. Let the benefits of economic growth bless both workers and investors, because both contribute to that growth, and both bear the risks of change in a dynamic economy.

Many people thought that after the lessons learned in financial crisis of the 1930's, no such disaster could ever happen again. Now the disaster has happened again. There is no guarantee that once the current crisis is over, we will be done with financial catastrophe forever. But the church can stand resolute for honest and prudent behavior, consistent with God's will for society, and maybe we can avoid such problems for a long time to come.

PART 3

ECONOMY AND ENVIRONMENT

10

Wasting Time and Wasting the Earth

INTRODUCTION

WE HAVE ALL KINDS of reasons for the environmental policies we have, but for many people it involves the intrinsic value of nature, apart from any use humans may make of it. That is not to say that we have no economic reasons for wanting to protect it. The benefits that come from the sustainable use of natural resources, the potentialities represented by biodiversity, and the aesthetic and recreational values of the outdoor world, all have value for us. We are interested in protecting the possibilities for future generations to use, appreciate, and benefit from the natural world. We want to use cost-effective means in pursuing our goal of protecting the integrity of nature. But it is not primarily about human economic use. For the vast majority of Americans of all faiths, environmental policy in general has more to do with the integrity of the natural world than utility or economics. That is why many environmental laws and policies actually forbid the use of cost-benefit analysis in their implementation. That is why we set aside inviolable environmental preserves that will be visited by very few people. This principle of intrinsic value is behind policies that call for "prevention of significant deterioration" of air and water quality. (Sagoff 1988, DeWitt 1998)

Considered as environmental policy then, recycling is a little odd, because it is almost always justified in purely economic terms. We encourage the recycling of trash, and do it ourselves even when it is personally costly to us, because it is supposed to save resources somewhere in the system. By saving economic resources through recycling, we make economic activity more sustainable, protecting future generations from an economic collapse brought about by resource scarcity. If we merely bury or burn our trash, this profligate use of resources will cause future generations to have to pay more to wrest materials from the ground, or pay for exhorbitantly priced substitutes. Besides, it just seems wasteful to throw away materials that look like they could be easily converted to new goods, and then go to all the effort to make those goods from the raw ores straight from the earth. That goes against most people's well-cultivated frugality.

PRICES AND THE EFFICIENCY OF RECYCLING

What makes this economic justification of recycling problematical is that, for the most part, recycling doesn't pay. (For some polemical statements of such results, see Tierney 1996; Boerner and Chilton 1994; Schaumburg and Doyle 1994. See also replies such as Denison and Ruston 1997; Consumer Reports 1994; and Ackerman 1997.) If recycling indeed saves resources, it should be less expensive, in strictly pecuniary terms, than the alternative of virgin materials production, single use, and landfilling. Except in a few rare cases, it is not, and that's what I mean when I say it doesn't pay. In no case does recycling of household waste pay in the sense that revenue from selling recovered materials covers all the costs of waste collection, separation, and marketing. (Duston 1993) If prices in some basic way reflect the scarcity of resources, the fact that recycling doesn't pay signals us that resources are not being saved in the recycling process, but rather some resources are indeed being wasted. Using prices to indicate scarcity makes sense in this case, at least as the first cut, because so many different resources are involved in this process, and somehow we must take account of and compare all of them. Virgin materials must be extracted from the ground, transported long distances, and be refined to be used. Recycled materials must be picked up and transported, separated from other materials and trash, and processed in with special equipment. So the pecuniary values should indicate which approach makes more economic sense. Economists especially would take this to be at the very least a rebuttable presumption.

So how could the presumption be rebutted? The claim could be made that in the case of recyclable materials, the prices are wrong, so they do not basically reflect the scarcity of resources for reasons peculiar to the materials involved. It could be the case that the production of virgin materials is subsidized, while recycled materials are not subsidized, so resources are being saved even though recycling does not save money. It was long the case that wood fiber from the national forests was sold for below-market stumpage rates, though this practice has been reformed to some degree by the Clinton administration. So wood and especially paper made from virgin pulp would be too cheap to really reflect scarcity. The production of crude oil and metal ores is subject to favorable income-tax treatment because of the depletion allowances and the expensing of mine development costs, though the 1986 tax reforms reduced these tax subsidies to some degree. In the bad old days of the Interstate Commerce Commission, regulated transportation rates favored bulk extractive commodities over manufactured goods or recycled materials, but the nearly complete deregulation of transportation means that these prices now are thoroughly reflective of costs. Though these subsidies were introduced for economic development reasons, it is now time to recognize that they lead to inefficiency in the economy, and they need to be eliminated. Gradually it seems that this is taking place.

To the extent that the extractive industries are not required to pay for the environmental damage caused by their activities, the prices of virgin materials will also be too low to reflect scarcity correctly. This was certainly the case for many years. These days if you suggest that it is still the case, you will get vociferous objections from people in those industries. The environmental requirements now placed on miners and loggers are very tough and very costly. Environmental and safety regulation is blamed for the fact that productivity growth in the extractive industries was quite slow throughout the 1970's and 1980's. (Rapid technological change has reversed this trend more recently.) It is only after titanic political struggles that the government succeeded in imposing these costs on industry. We are much closer than we were to a system in which the environmental costs of virgin resource extraction are fully incorporated in the prices of the products we use.

Another way in which prices could be wrong has to do with the way we price waste-disposal services. If landfill space is more scarce than the prices suggest, because future landfill sites are very limited in availability, or if landfill tipping fees do not fully reflect the environmental impact of landfilling, that would tend to make recycling look less economical than in fact it is. At $50/ton for landfilling, it is hard to make recycling pay, while at $90/ton, recycling almost always pays. (Williams 1991) (Profitability also depends on extractive commodity prices, which are quite volatile. Since the middle-1990's, they have been very low by historical standards.) When landfill tipping fees were administered by government agencies, and landfills were basically unregulated, it was easier to make this case. Now the environmental impact of landfills is highly regulated, and modern landfills are constructed to be nearly completely sealed off from the natural environment, and monitored to make sure they stay that way. Landfills now are often owned by private waste-disposal companies, rather than by governments, and haulers are encouraged to find the cheapest place to go. Tipping fees therefore are no longer adminstered prices, but are set in a reasonably competitive market, and should therefore fully reflect site availability. And they are still in the $40–50 per ton range.

If households or businesses face a zero price for added volumes of waste, it also creates a problem for recycling. How waste disposal is priced to the ultimate customers makes no difference to the calculation about whether recycling pays, but it does affect the incentives people face, and consequently their behavior. With no additional cost for additional trash, people not only have no incentive to save money by putting waste in the recycling bin instead of the trash, but they also have no incentive to reduce the total amount of waste that they generate. Economists have tended to focus on this pricing discrepancy as the root of the recycling problem. The best work suggests that we should put a tax on materials at a level that would reflect the damage done by littering, and then offer free trash pickup and pay people to recycle. Such a system includes incentives to minimize waste materials and to recycle, and avoids giving people an incentive to litter by making trash collection free. In some respects, this resembles the deposit-return system that is frequently used for beverage containers, a system that should be considered for wider applications. (Fullerton and Kinnaman 1995)

But while this tax-subsidy program is a theoretically elegant approach to the problem, and one that is well suited to the analytical tools of the economics discipline, it is not likely to make much practical difference. The price levels we are talking about for disposing of trash are very modest, on the order of a couple of dollars a week, and the effect of these prices on behavior seems to be very weak. (Reschovsky and Stone 1994; Miranda et al. 1994; Morris and Holthausen 1994; Palmer et al. 1997; Ackerman 1997) Most managers of recycling programs have found that to increase recycling, the most important thing to do is to make it as convenient as possible, offering frequent pickups, free containers, and demanding as little source separation as possible. In addition, there has to be an ongoing communication and marketing program, to maintain the level of interest, awareness, and compliance. (Lansana et. al. 1991; Carroll 1995)

So, while prices are not exactly right, after several decades of increasing environmental regulation, transportation deregulation, and tax reform, the prices do not seem to be very far wrong. Charging for trash pickup would increase littering as well as inducing material reduction, reuse and recycling, so on balance probably is not a good idea. There is a case for stiffer severance taxes on virgin materials. A high tax on petroleum would not only raise the cost of plastic, which is hard to landfill or recycle, but also discourage carbon emissions, a good thing all the way around. As many economists point out, this kind of tax increases economic efficiency and sustainability, and so is hands-down superior to taxes on wages or incomes, which reduce efficiency. But as the fate of President Clinton's carbon and BTU tax proposals suggests, the political world doesn't seem to be ready for such tax reform moves yet. The one virtue that can be claimed for the extremely regressive sales taxes that most states employ is that they are mostly taxes on tangible goods, and so discourage the material throughput of the economy. We need to keep making the case for a tax system that is environmentally (and economically) based.

WHICH RESOURCES, WHAT WASTE?

Advocates of recycling make their case by stressing the resources that are saved in the process. Recycling above all saves energy. Though energy is expended in the process of collecting and transporting recyclable materials, this expenditure is very modest if the system is managed properly so that recycling collections substitute for trash collections to a large degree. Of course, virgin materials have to be transported too, sometimes over great distances from remote mines or forests. Much energy is saved in the manufacturing process. This is most dramatically the case for aluminum, the material that brings in the most revenue for recycling programs, but it is also the case for glass, paper, and even plastic. (Williams 1991)

Extractive resources are also saved. In some cases these are non-renewable resources, like metal ores or crude oil feedstock. In these cases, sustainability alone suggests that recycling is not only desirable, but necessary. Yes, there are theoretically renewable substitutes for crude oil feedstock, such as vegetable oils, but there is a cost attached to that also. The fact that renewable feedstock is nowhere used to produce plastic tells us something about the technical difficulty and economic cost of this approach. The wood fiber that goes into paper production is of course a renewable resource, but lurking behind the interest in paper recycling is concern about the destruction of standing forest ecosystems, which provide benefits in terms of biodiversity, wildlife habitat, carbon sequestration, and watershed management. Not all of these benefits can be retained in forest systems even when they are sustainably managed for fiber production. So the broader sustainability question is an issue even for wood fiber recycling.

If energy and extractive resources are indeed being saved in the recycling process, what resource is being used to such an extent that recycling is more expensive than burying or burning the trash? Labor. Human work. Recycling, especially recovery of recyclable materials from the waste stream, is a very labor-intensive activity. This has long been a source of great frustration, if not to recycling advocates, at least to the managers of recycling programs in the private and public sectors, who must remove society's waste on a budget. A lot of effort has gone into the project of automating the materials recovery system. (Stessel 1996) But walk into any random materials recovery facility (called in the trade an MRF or "murf") and you will see a few simple machines, like a magnet, a trommel, and an air separator, surrounding a crew of people dressed in hats, gloves, and dust masks, picking through the trash as it comes by on a conveyor belt. It is depressingly low-tech, dirty, uncomfortable, and somewhat dangerous work. It is often the job of prisoners (in municipal facilities), sheltered workshop participants, or recent immigrants, which is to say it doesn't pay very well. But payroll is more than half the cost involved in running a MRF, and the MRF is what makes recycling so expensive.

In fact, recycling by businesses is usually profitable precisely because their recyclables do not have to be processed at a MRF. Manufacturers' lines produce scrap which can be collected and sold to scrap dealers or upstream manufacturers without having to be separated from household trash. It may go to a MRF if the company doesn't want to handle the transportation and brokerage itself, but it doesn't go through the pickers' line, and the privately-owned MRF makes money on it. The company producing it sometimes has a concern about sustainability or social efficiency that motivates its recycling program, but the programs are usually profitable (which is to say less expensive than the alternative of trashing the scrap) whatever the motivation. Office paper recycling programs are usually profitable also. Separation is done at the source by office workers who deposit waste paper into recycling bins instead of an all-purpose trash can, and the resulting material can be sold for premium prices to waste hauling companies or scrap brokers, and be used by paper manufacturers without further processing. The offices do not cost out any extra time for their employees to do this separation work. It is rather treated as a systems change that results in increased worker productivity. The only cost the businesses worry about is the containers, but that is a modest expense, quickly recovered by the profitability of the program. (This also suggests that it makes no sense to count household sorting time as a cost of recycling. If profit-making businesses don't consider it significant, why should a cost-benefit analysis count it against household recycling? See also Denison and Ruston 1997 and Ackerman 1997.)

Recycling proponents sometimes try to make a virtue out of this necessity of labor-intensive sorting of household recyclables. The claim is that recycling creates jobs, and thus could be an important contributor to economic development. Several considerations make this claim suspect. First, the jobs created in the MRF's are not very good jobs, as we have seen. Second, they are jobs that have to be subsidized, either by taxpayers in the case of municipal MRF's, or by business-oriented recycling programs in the case of the private sector. These are not productive jobs in the usual economic sense of the word. They do not create economic value in the form of output that people are willing to pay for. We might want to subsidize jobs during a recession in order to ameliorate the social and economic problems that come with mass unemployment. But the jobs connected with recycling can not be turned on and off according to the state of the business cycle. If the private sector is to invest in the durable machinery needed to use recyclable resources, there must be a consistent supply of recycled material. After a shaky start, there has been a lot of success on this score in the last ten years. Making jobs on the MRF line employment of last resort during recessions would undo that progress.

The deeper issue has to do with how we think about different categories of resources. To economists, all resources are comparable in terms of their prices. The claim that recycling saves resources can only mean that recycling is less expensive than landfilling or other alternative trash disposal techniques when all the costs are considered. Energy, primary ores, wood fiber, biodiversity, clean water, and labor are all costed out at their market prices, or some synthetic substitute for market prices, and compared. This approach does not recognize any distinction between different kinds of resources, particularly labor and energy. Some of those distinctions may be important for sustainability, for health and safety, and for the intrinsic value of nature. But the virtue of this approach is that it allows us to compare incomparable things ("apples and oranges"), which we have to do to understand a process as complicated as recycling. At some stage we have to make those comparisons, because we cannot attribute absolute value to nature, or to energy conservation, without absolutely devaluing human life, and that's not the point of doing this.

The implicit message of the recycling proponents is that it is possible to waste energy, and it is possible to waste extractive resources, but it is not possible to waste human time and effort. All jobs are worth doing, especially any job that uses human effort to save some natural resource. This approach recognizes some distinctions that are important. Human life and labor is renewable in a way that even wood fiber is not. Drawing more people into work on environmental issues and causes does not damage the environment in the way that cutting a standing forest does. (We would not want to say that a larger population does not have a detrimental impact on the environment.) But this argument can easily be carried too far. In the extreme, we could go back to a world of human hunters and gatherers living in an equilibrium with natural ecosystems, but then we give up all the advantages of culture. (Some small groups of anarchists favor this, but it is an extreme view.) And not all of our interventions on behalf of environmental protection work out the way we intend. Sometimes our efforts to control nature, even to make it more sustainable or "natural," turn out to be futile or counterproductive. For instance, protecting the national parks against any and all forest fires turned out to be a mistake. Less can be more. Nature changes, and we don't always know enough to guide that change intelligently.

But what about recycling? Is it worth the effort? I would say that it is, but not for strictly economic reasons. The argument goes very much like any debate over a line item in the local government budget. Should we hire a small crew of people to clean up and maintain the local parks, or should we rely on volunteers? How much should we spend on it? How nice can we afford to make the parks? The issue with recycling is the same. We know that recycling has environmental benefits like energy (fossil fuel) savings, reduced mining and logging, reduced demand for landfilling and incineration, and enhanced sustainability. It is an expression of our respect for the integrity of God's Creation. How much are we willing to pay for those environmental benefits? How much should we appropriate for that line in the municipal budget? I think that once we cast the recycling issue in these clearly environmental terms, we can have a sensible debate about it. My own view is that the cost of household recycling is very modest compare to the considerable environmental benefits to be had. I recognize that other people may disagree with my judgement on this matter. But cost-benefit analysis showing that recycling does not save resources in the conventional economic sense does not close the issue. (Robison 1994)

Though waste collection has usually been a local-government responsibility in the U.S., it may make more sense to carry on the debate at the state level. Cities or even counties may not be able to provide a large enough supply of recyclable material to induce the complementary private sector investments in manufacturing facilities that are necessary to make a market for recyclables. The scale of the required subsidies might be less intimidating in the context of a state budget than in a closely-balanced, property-tax-based local budget. A creative state-wide program can provide support for creative, well organized and managed efforts at the local level. (Callan and Thomas 1997) Still, there are many areas of the country where effective recycling programs exist without a statewide mandate or subsidies, and the overall supply of recyclable materials has not been a barrier to the development of an extensive network of recycling-based manufacturing facilities. (Powelson and Powelson 1992)

Of course, reduction of waste and reuse of products are better than recycling. Reduction of waste (without a decline in living standards) has all the environmental benefits of recycling, plus the economic benefit that it really does save resources, because nothing has to be laboriously hand-sorted at the MRF. There is some evidence that our economy is becoming more efficient in this sense. The physical weight of the average dollar of GDP is declining, as Federal Reserve Chair Alan Greenspan never tires of remarking. New materials and the technology of miniaturization have helped us do more with less. What raises questions for people are those cases where excessive packaging has been provided as a substitute for inconvenience, especially with foods. We have to remember that what looks like excessive packaging sometimes reduces the waste of food, which is itself a worthwhile goal. A lot more material reduction could be achieved by getting prices closer to right levels. As for reuse, three cheers for thrift stores and garage sales! All the benefits with hardly any costs.

MAKING RECYCLING WORK

For household recycling to work, it must have the support of the users of the service. Householders must accept a pickup schedule that substitutes recyclables pickup for ordinary trash runs, if collection costs are to be kept under control. Smart recycling managers try to make recycling as simple as possible, but controlling MRF costs demands a certain amount and quality of source separation. Of course, the additional costs of recycling have to be met out of tax revenues, for which public support is also necessary.

All of this means that there must be an ongoing communication effort, not only to inform households of what they need to do to make the program work, but to maintain overall support for the effort. The publicity that has been given to recent cost-benefit studies has undercut the economic case for recycling. Householders need to be convinced of the benefits of recycling based on its environmental benefits. If the case is made in environmental, rather than economic, terms, I believe the public will be far more receptive to continuation or even expansion of the recycling effort, and a higher level of cooperation will make the programs work better and cost less.

Recycling has become an important topic in environmental education in the primary schools. Very often it is the children who have responsibility for sorting and taking out the household trash, and they are often also the most knowlegeable and supportive members of the household. Many apartment and condominium communities have recycling programs because the children demand it. Otherwise there are often problems implementing recycling where many people share common trash and recycling recepticles. Compliance suffers when individual households cannot be held accountable for their behavior. (Gandy 1993)

Businesses have an easier job of it, because businesses' recycling usually pays. Still, good management techniques must be used to maintain a high-quality, low-cost program. Top management must make a strong and visible commitment to the program as integral to the mission of the business. All of the tools necessary to proper functioning of the program have to be easily available to all the workers, and supervisors must be committed to keeping the requirements of the program in front of their workers and continuously evaluating compliance. The program must be a regular part of employee training and must be featured often in internal communications. Where programs have this level of management support they usually succeed and save companies money. On the other hand, if the top management of the company constantly questions the benefits of the program, or vocally worries about the cost, compliance will deteriorate over time. As compliance deteriorates, quality of separation will decline, the recyclables will bring lower prices from the brokers, and the costs of the program will increase. (Berman 1996)

Many economists would be willing to predict that in the future it will become easier to make the case for recycling on economic grounds. It seems very likely that the price of landfill space will increase in the future. Suitable land will be more scarce and more remotely located as cities expand and residents become more sensitive to the noxious spillover effects from these dumps. Regulations to control the overall environmental impact of landfills will only become tighter, and compliance more expensive. The prediction of commodity prices is an uncertain business, and no economist would stake a career on a prediction concerning the long-term trend of commodity prices. Still, nearly everybody believes that commodity prices are currently at unusually low levels, reflecting the temporarily depressed circumstances of the east Asian and central European economies. We are likely to see significantly higher prices for virgin raw materials, and consequently for recycled materials, in future, more normal times. But we must not abandon the strictly environmental arguments for recycling when it returns to profitability in the future, because economic conditions could change again. It is important that the effort be maintained so that the complementary private sector investments in manufacturing capacity are also maintained.

CONCLUSION

It is not wrong to do things for economic reasons. In fact, the stewardship of Creation demands that we not waste resources. Ordinarily, being "economical," doing with less, is also the environmentally responsible thing to do. It is a curious anomaly when economic stewardship (considered in its broadest context, not a narrow individualistic one) and environmental responsibility call for different actions. In this paper, I suggest that recycling is one of those anomalous cases.

The reason that the economic calculation comes out wrong in this case is that the resource being "wasted" is human labor. That is, recycling substitutes labor for natural resource commodities like metal ores, crude oil, and pulpwood. This is an acceptable substitution, not because human labor is worthless, or because it is impossible to waste people's time, or because the jobs in Materials Recovery Facilities have such great intrinsic worth, but because the environmental benefits of recycling make it worth the effort and expense. This is a qualitative judgement, of the sort we make every day when we make budgets, and can neither be supported or refuted by resort to a strict cost-benefit analysis or some other mathematical formula.

The decision that recycling is worth the cost is also informed by the prediction or expectation that recycling will turn out to be justifiable in strictly economic terms and landfilling becomes a steadily more expensive and less attractive alternative, and as natural resource commodity prices bounce back from what seem to be abnormally depressed levels. The fixed nature of private-sector investment in the manufacturing facilities that are complementary to the recycling effort means that the effort needs to be consistent, even though the profitability of recycling itself is not consistent.

It would be easier to make the economic case for recycling if the fiscal authorities made more use of taxes on virgin extractive commodities to make their prices reflect all the environmental costs connected with their production and use. This is especially true of crude oil. Oil is the raw material for making plastics, an increasing share of our wastes and a difficult material to recycle. As a fossil fuel, it is also the major source of carbon emissions which contribute to climate change. A stiff tax on crude oil, coupled with reductions in payroll taxes, would make the economy function more efficiently, discouraging environmental degradation and encouraging employment. It would also make the economics of recycling more clearly reflect its overall benefits.

REFERENCES

Ackerman, Frank. 1997. *Why Do We Recycle? Markets, Values, and Public Policy.* Washington: Island.

Berman, Fran. 1996. *Trash to Cash: How Businesses Can Save Money and Increase Profits.* Delray Beach, FL: St. Lucie.

Boerner, Christopher, and Kenneth Chilton. 1994. "False Economy: The Folly of Demand-Side Recycling." *Environment* (January/February) 6ff.

Callan, Scott J., and Janet M. Thomas. 1997. "The Impact of State and Local Policies on the Recycling Effort." *Eastern Economic Journal* (Fall) 411–23.

Carroll, Wayne. 1995. "The Organization and Efficiency of Residential Recycling Services." *Eastern Economic Journal* (Spring) 215–25.

Consumer Reports editors. 1994. "Recycling: Is It Worth The Effort?" *Consumer Reports* (Feb.) 92–8.

Denison, Richard A., and John F. Ruston. 1997. "Recycling Is Not Garbage." *Technology Review* (October) 55–60.

DeWitt, Calvin B. 1998. *Caring for Creation: Responsible Stewardship of God's Handiwork.* Grand Rapids: Baker.

Duston, Thomas E. 1993. *Recycling Solid Waste: The First Choice for Private and Public Sector Management.* Westport, CT: Quorum.

Fullerton, Don, and Thomas C. Kinnaman. 1995. "Garbage, Recycling, and Illicit Burning or Dumping." *Journal of Environmental Economics and Management* (July) 78–91.

Gandy, Matthew. 1993. *Recycling and Waste: An Exploration of Contemporary Environmental Policy.* Aldershot, UK: Avebury.

Lansana, Florence M., Milton E. Harvey, and John W. Frazier. 1991. "Recycling Behavior: The Causal Role of Demographic, Communication, and Attitudinal Factors." in *Energy, the Environment, and Public Policy: Issues for the 1990's.* Greenwood: Praeger. 78–88.

Miranda, Marie Lynn, Jess W. Everett, Daniel Blume, and Barbeau A. Roy, Jr. 1994. "Market-Based Incentives and Residential Municipal Solid Waste." *Journal of Policy Analysis and Management* (Fall) 681–98.

Morris, Glenn E., and Duncan M. Holthausen, Jr. 1994. "The Economics of Household Solid Waste Generation and Disposal." *Journal of Environmental Economics and Management.* (May) 215–35.

Palmer, Karen, Hilary Sigman, and Margaret Walls. 1997. "The Cost of Reducing Municipal Solid Waste." *Journal of Environmental Economics and Management* (June) 128–50.

Powelson, David R., and Melinda A. Powelson. 1992. *The Recycler's Manual for Business, Government, and the Environmental Community.* New York: Van Nostrand Reinhold.

Reschovsky, James D., and Sarah E. Stone. 1994. "Market Incentives to Encourage Household Waste Recycling." *Journal of Policy Analysis and Management* (Winter) 120–39.

Robison, Wade L. 1994. *Decisions in Doubt: The Environment and Public Policy.* Hanover, NH: University Press of New England.

Sagoff, Mark. 1988. *The Economy of the Earth: Philosophy, Law, and the Environment.* Cambridge: Cambridge University Press.

Schaumburg, Grant W. Jr., and Katherine T. Doyle. 1994. "Forced Recycling Costs Consumers." *Consumers' Research* (April) 30–32.

Stessel, Richard I. 1996. *Recycling and Resource Recovery Engineering.* Berlin: Springer.

Tierney, John. 1996. "Recycling Is Garbage." *New York Times Magazine* (June 30) 24ff.

Williams, Susan. 1991. *Trash to Cash: New Business Opportunities in the Post-Consumer Waste Stream.* Washington: Investor Responsibility Research Center.

11

Environmental Policy for Business and Government

OPTIONS FOR POLICY

ECONOMISTS OFFER A LONG list of policy options for dealing with environmental problems. Most involve ways of designing government interventions. They include emission fees, marketable permits, quantitative limits, technological mandates, and various forms of subsidies. In the spirit of the Coase Theorem, there are also different ways for government to assign and enforce property rights for environmental goods, to encourage private negotiations to resolve environmental problems. Much of the literature in environmental economics is devoted to establishing which each of these interventions works best under various special circumstances.

However, it is clear from this literature that government interventions sometimes do not work very well, no matter how cleverly they are designed. There is also a great deal of dissatisfaction with government environmental policy in practice. A great deal of the professional business literature, as well as frequent news reports, suggest that many if not most businesses have their own environmental policies that go well beyond mere compliance with government mandates or response to external incentives. (See e.g. Shelton, 1995, or Krol, 1995.) The environment is too big an issue to be effectively managed by government alone, and the private business sector is responding to the growth of public concern about the sustainability of economic activity.

The questions addressed in this paper have to do with the division of responsibility for environmental care between government policy intervention and private business policy initiative. Which aspects of environmental concern are best dealt with by the various government policy devices, and which are better left to be dealt with by businesses operating under their own responsibility? How can government encourage businesses to develop sound environmental policies? How should academic economists, ethicists, and business professionals, as well as other public intellectuals, encourage responsible environmental policies and practices by businesses?

THE CONTEXT OF BUSINESS POLICY

In posing these questions, I am assuming that there will be a responsive audience in the business community. In elementary economic theory, and among some Chicago School economists, it is argued that profit-maximizing firms in competitive markets effectively have no choices when it comes to business practices or production technology. A firm that does not choose the unique cost-minimizing combination of inputs and the unique vector of profit-maximizing outputs will be put out of business by its rivals, or else liquidated or merged out of existence by disgruntled shareholders. There is therefore no room for businesses to make independent decisions about environmental care.

For business choices about environmental policy to make any difference at all, it is sufficient that markets not be perfectly competitive, so that firms with different technologies and costs, and differentiated products, can coexist. Alternatively, it could be the case that the managers and owners of the firm have values beyond the maximization of their own material well-being, values which might include environmental sustainability. A developing social consensus about the environment could cause all businesses to institute environmental policies that would still keep all of them on a level playing field Mounting evidence from experimental studies of game-theoretic issues show that agents who are perceived as moral and trustworthy develop business advantages over rivals that condone opportunistic behavior (Frank 1996). All of these considerations suggest that the elementary conclusion of the irrelevance of business policy is not correct under realistic conditions. The reports cited above concerning business environmental initiatives provide empirical confirmation.

To understand what aspects of the issue will find a good reception in the business community, it is important to understand the motivations managers have for developing environmental policies (Harford, 1997; Smith, 1993; Shelton, 1995; and Krol, 1995). Managers wish to act preemptively on the environment in order to retain control of the issue, and if possible to forestall further regulatory action or lawsuits. There are more and more examples of businesses that have adopted the philosophy of waste reduction: any material leaving the plant represents waste, and reducing these emissions or solid waste removals is an opportunity to reduce production costs by making using more of the material that comes into the plant. By rethinking production technology in the light of this philosophy, all forms of pollution can be reduced, forestalling any need for regulation. Pollution can be reduced in a way that reduces costs, which is often not possible when regulation mandates particular technological fixes or end-of-pipe solutions. Profitability is the bottom line here; nevertheless, the waste-reduction principle is a radical change in business philosophy, and moves in the direction of the environmental movement.

Building goodwill in the community by being environmentally responsible, and appearing so, has other positive consequences for companies. When they present information on other public issues, their credibility is greater, so they are more likely to be believed, and their position is more likely to be taken seriously and to prevail. They are less likely to be the target of aggressive regulatory action, or investigation by public agencies or the press. Environmentally responsible businesses are likely to have a marketing advantage with many potential customers who hold strong environmentalist views. All of these matters again speak to the long-run prosperity of the firm, but that is a recognition that it will be necessary for organizations to adapt in order to survive in the future in a world that is increasingly aware of environmental issues and governed by environmental principles.

Most business managers understand that they run organizations that are embedded in a society in which certain mores are taken for granted. Indeed, most managers have their own moral convictions that govern their lives. It would be rather strange if well-meaning, well-educated managers exhibited so little integrity or sensitivity that they regularly flouted conventional moral standards. Such standards change over time, sometimes for the better and sometimes for the worse. Once it was considered impolite to ask somebody to extinguish their cigarette; now hardly any businesses even permit smoking on their premises. Nearly everyone agrees this is a change for the better. On the other hand, price discrimination that once would have been morally suspect is now considered normal and appropriate (e.g., airline fares or frequent buyer plans). Environmental standards for business are rising dramatically. For example, an office-paper recycling program was once rare, but is now expected in all establishments, and its absence is rapidly coming to be considered morally questionable.

This is as it should be. In business, as in all other areas of life, some actions are morally right and others are morally wrong. The question of what is right to do cannot always be answered by reference to the principles of maximizing shareholder value and meeting the competition. Managers are required to consider other ethical principles as well. Morality is not the exclusive province of a benign, social-welfare-maximizing government. The ethical principle of sustainability binds both business and government, and the point of this paper is to apply that principle in a way that can be practically useful to business, and productive in explaining business behavior. When economists ignore the ethical bases of business behavior, they make their discipline increasingly irrelevant. The stakes involved in environmental ethics are very large and growing.

THE AREAS OF GOVERNMENT RESPONSIBILITY

Economic analysis would suggest that the areas in which government policy instruments would work best would be where the environmental good in question has the nature of a public good. These would include the traditional types of pollution problems, where there are many sources of the pollutant, many parties who suffer the consequences of the pollution, and the total amount of pollution is crucial to the amount of damage done. It is for these conditions that the economists' favorite policy instruments are intended: emission fees and marketable emission permits. These kinds of pollution problems are the ones that governments have had the most success solving.

In most of these large-numbers cases, the pollution problem encompasses a wide geographic area, and so necessarily involves government at the national or international level. Politicians often prefer that more localized pollution problems be handled at a lower level of government, where the people who suffer from the problem have a more direct voice, and national office-holders are not on the spot, but this poses difficulties of its own. If there are only a handful of pollution sources, the economic incentives for decentralized decision-making are beside the point. Furthermore, large businesses can have a great deal of power over smaller local government bodies. Simply by threatening to move, the business can often have its way. While such a situation may seem to demand involvement of a higher government level, it also raises an opportunity for businesses themselves to take hold of the problem.

The most controversial and least successful of the national environmental laws and policies have mostly to do with very localized problems: the superfund act, the regulation of toxic substances (e.g., the benzene standard), and the Endangered Species Act. Besides localized effects, these problems share the characteristic that each instance of the problem presents unique features which enforcement must take into account. There is no common substance whose total amount has to be kept below some threshold—rather, each case is a completely new regulatory problem. Negotiation between government and business is often a feature of these situations, and business responsibility has to play a role in cost-effective control of these problems.

Where government does best, then, is regulating the conventional pollution of regional and international airsheds, large surface bodies of water, and large aquifers. Policy tools based on economic incentives and decentralized decision-making work well in these cases. Other kinds of environmental issues do not have the public goods characteristics that make government intervention productive.

THE AREAS OF BUSINESS RESPONSIBILITY

Business responsibility for pollution problems is crucial where the external effects are localized and the pollution sources are few. Regulation is difficult in such cases because of the economic power that enterprises have in a local community. The national authorities are not interested, and incentive programs are unnecessarily complicated. On the other hand, a business that holds itself out as environmentally responsible can easily be held publicly accountable in such cases. Pollution problems are immediately noticeable, and who else is there to blame for the pollution?

Wetlands, habitats of endangered species, and other environmentally sensitive lands pose similar issues. Spillover effects are mostly localized, and land use is traditionally regulated at the local level, but developers wield significant local political power. Federal-level regulation has mostly failed. Setting aside land by having government or some private group like the Nature Conservancy buy it is not always possible or desirable. However, a business that has environmental sustainability as a policy objective can be held accountable, as the media and private environmental organizations can investigate or monitor performance (Owen, 1992, ch. 5, and Turcotte, 1995).

Non-point pollution sources pose difficult problems when approached with the conventional policy tools. Since it is difficult to measure actual emissions, strategies based on emission amounts do not work in the ways they are intended. Estimates of emission amounts are based on materials use and technology, so in effect these emission fees or permits turn into technology standards. Sometimes technological upgrades are required or subsidized, but such programs do not necessarily lead to efficient maintenance and operation of the process to reduce emissions. Therefore, business responsibility is necessarily involved in controlling non-point emissions.

The regulation of the use and disposal of toxic substances has been an area where government performance has been disappointing. The large number and variety of such substances in industrial use, and the necessity of giving businesses some flexibility in the introduction and use of such substances, has made their regulation really impractical. The most useful thing that government has been able to do is to require disclosure of information about the use and disposal of these materials. This does not force companies to handle them in a safe manner, but it does mean that companies with strong environmental and safety policies can be held accountable by unions, journalists, and other private groups.

Disclosure requirements are also useful in the area of environmental marketing. Requiring businesses to disclose to their customers and to the public the environmental and safety characteristics of their products does not automatically improve the products. But it does provide the business with an occasion to use the information in marketing their products to consumers who are concerned about the environment. Companies can change products to stand up more favorably on the disclosed measures, and can inform the public about the importance of the related environmental issues. It requires initiative by the company, but the mechanism for accountability is present. (See Karl and Orwat, 2000.)

Business responsibility coupled with disclosure requirements may be the best way to handle situations where technological change is particularly rapid. It is often argued that one advantage of using effluent fees or permits is that they don't require policies to change when technology changes. However, if technological change shifts the pollution-control cost function, the efficient pollution level may change, requiring a change in the fee or the number of permits (unless there are strong threshold effects). Businesses can make these adjustments much more rapidly and effectively than government can. Especially where product technology is concerned, requiring businesses to disclose environmental performance can stimulate the introduction of newer, cleaner, and safer technology.

ENCOURAGING ENVIRONMENTAL INITIATIVES BY BUSINESS

Government plays an important role in encouraging business environmental responsibility by requiring disclosure of information about businesses' environmental performance. These requirements open up the possibility for holding businesses publicly accountable for meeting goals. Government can and does also encourage businesses to work together to develop new technologies, both by sponsoring industry consortia and by subsidizing research.

However, I think it is too much to expect elected officials to take the lead in developing the ethical case for action, leading the development of a public consensus, in setting environmental goals for industry, or calling for action. While an elected official with a public mandate can be effective in developing public policy, there have been too many public moral and intellectual lapses by our public leadership, going back to the days of Vietnam and Watergate, for these officials to have the credibility to lead in this area. Furthermore, there is a history of adversarial relations between business and government on the environmental issue in particular that makes it unlikely that government leadership would work.

The task of building moral consensus and encouraging business initiatives falls more properly and more practically to the moral-cultural or civil sector of society— academics, journalists, environmental activists, church leaders, and public intellectuals. These are the people who are best equipped to make the case, who have access to media and opinion leaders, and who have the independent credibility necessary to lead on this issue (See Shrivastava, 1995).

Business and government leaders can join in this process by reiterating the arguments made by civil-society leaders whose positions they find agreeable, and by engaging the arguments they disagree with. The mistakes that government and business officials often make in dealing with civil organizations are to question the representative nature of the organizations (How many members does your group have?), and to question the motives of leaders (Aren't you just trying to get new members, grant money, or jury awards in tort cases?). In public discussion of this kind, the important thing is to engage the ideas, not to question the motives or the credibility of the proponents. *Ad hominem* arguments are not ethical, and the public loses patience with politicians and business people who make them. Similarly, environmental groups that are reflexively anti-business do not gain credibility with the public. A cooperative spirit is the key to success. (See Winn, 1995)

CONCLUSION

Civil society leaders and, to a lesser extent, politicians can lead the way in developing the moral case for a sustainable economy. Persuading business leaders of the importance of business environmental initiatives is a key step toward business assuming responsibility in this area.

Public discussion of these issues also leads to the formation of a social consensus on environmental issues. With such a consensus in place, businesses that undertake environmental initiatives are less likely to be penalized in market competition. Recognizing this consensus, political leaders can introduce requirements for businesses to disclose their environmental performance. Journalists and activists can then use this information to hold businesses accountable to social standards of environmental responsibility.

Holding individual businesses accountable for environmental performance is likely to work best where there are few, readily identifiable sources of the environmental problem and the environmental effects of the behavior are localized. It can also work well where the technology involved is unique to a particular plant or process, or where technology is rapidly changing. Businesses can also take advantage of opportunities for "green marketing" in cases where environmental characteristics of products are important, and delivering relevant information to environmentally conscious consumers would create a marketing advantage.

REFERENCES

Collins, Denis, and Mark Starik, eds. 1995. *Sustaining the Natural Environment: Empirical Studies on the Interface Between Nature and Organizations*. Research in Corporate Social Performance and Policy, Supplement 1. Greenwich, CT: JAI.

Frank, Robert H. 1996. "Can Socially Responsible Firms Survive in a Competitive Environment?" In David M. Messick and Ann E. Tenbrunsel, eds., *Codes of Conduct: Behavioral Research into Business Ethics*. New York: Russell Sage Foundation.

Harford, Jon D. 1997. "Firm Ownership Patterns and Motives for Voluntary Pollution Control," *Managerial and Decision Economics* 18 (6) 421–31.

Karl, Helmut, and Carsten Orwat. 2000. "Environmental Marketing and Public Policy," In Henk Folmer and H. Landis Gabel, eds., *Principles of Environmental and Resource Economics,* 2nd ed. Northampton, MA: Edward Elgar.

Krol, Andre. 1995. "Environmental Management—Issues and Approaches for an Organization." In Rogers, ed., 1995, 51–88.

Owen, Dave. 1992. *Green Reporting: Accountancy and the Challenge of the Nineties.* London: Chapman & Hall.

Rogers, Michael D., ed. 1995. *Business and the Environment.* New York: St. Martin's.

Shelton, Robert D. 1995. "The Greening of American Industry." In Rogers ed., 1995, 3–18.

Shrivastava, Paul. 1995. "Industrial/Environmental Crises and Corporate Social Responsibility." *Journal of Socio-Economics* 24 (1) 211–27.

Smith, Denis. (1993). "The Frankenstein Syndrome: Corporate Responsibility and the Environment." In Denis Smith, ed., *Business and the Environment: Implications of the New Environmentalism.* New York: St. Martin's, 172–89.

Turcotte, Marie-France. 1995. "Conflict and Collaboration: The Interfaces between Environmental Organizations and Business Firms." In Collins and Starik, eds., 1995, 195–229.

Winn, Monika I. 1995. "Corporate Leadership and Policies for the Natural Environment." In Collins and Starik, eds., 1995, 127–61.

12

Rethinking the Costs of Economic Growth

INTRODUCTION

WHEN YOU ARE A critic of the received wisdom in economics, as I am, at some point you have to stop and consider whether there is anything in the conventional approach to the subject that you think is actually right. Especially if teaching the subject is what pays your bills, it helps to have some part of the standard material that you can latch onto with enthusiasm, so your students don't think you are completely crazy. If you are constantly at war with the textbook and the syllabus, the students are apt to give up trying to understand anything at all. I probably waited too long to undertake this task, leaving it until I decided to write my own survey textbook to really examine my own beliefs.

The basic idea from mainstream economics that I think is right is the gains from trade theorem. I have come to believe that the key to economic development and growth, the key to the great escape from hunger, misery, and want, is comparative advantage, specialization, and exchange. The poorest people in the world are incredibly resourceful and hardworking. They grow their own food, build their own houses, make their own garments, educate their own children, treat their own illnesses, and they are dirt poor. The richest people in the world do the same thing over and over again, one coronary artery bypass surgery after another, one performance of the greatest hits after another, one contract drafted after another, all day every day, and they buy almost everything they need. The simple recognition of the value of specialization is most of what it takes to escape poverty.

I will consider first the reasons that specialization explains development and growth better than the other leading possibilities. Then, after a brief examination of past literature on the costs of growth, I want to give full attention to the negative consequences that specialization has for the economy and the society. I will then return to the issue of the desirability of growth, and how to avoid the problems it brings.

THE SOURCES OF ECONOMIC GROWTH

Capital accumulation alone can't account for the magnitude of growth (Helpman 2004, ch. 3). Most of the growth in per capita incomes is the result of total-factor productivity growth. Sometimes capital growth does no good at all. The commodity price revolution of the 1970's rendered a large part of the capital stock obsolete rather suddenly. The vast investment in desktop computers in the 1980's and early 1990's did little good until specialized software and networking finally sparked a productivity explosion (Gordon 2003). Until then, they were just very expensive typewriters. Capital for growth must be specialized tools to go with specialized labor, making use of knowledge of the state of the art. Woodworking hobbyists acquire rooms full of highly specialized, expensive hand tools that, placed in a modern factory, would retard productivity, not enhance it.

The mistaken idea that capital investment is the source of all growth lies at the bottom of much current policy debate. It is used to justify the idea that the growth dividend should not be shared with labor, but only with the stockholders. It is also used to justify the idea that income from capital should not be taxed, but the entire tax burden should be borne by labor (i.e. zero taxes on dividends, or the Roth IRA). Not only is this bad economics and bad social policy, but it also reverses the whole western philosophical tradition that favors work and wages, while casting suspicion on income gained from interest or speculative gain.

Usually the gains in total factor productivity are attributed to technological change (Helpman 2004, ch. 4). Economists have never found a satisfactory independent measure of technological change. Counting patent grants and totting up R&D spending have obvious limitations, and using productivity as a proxy assumes what we're trying to prove. Technology thus becomes the hand-waving expedient that can explain anything we want it to. But those of us in academic life get to see our science and engineering colleagues change technology close up, so we know what it is even if we can't measure it. Technological change is what happens when smart people apply themselves to solving very particular, narrow problems. This may mean bringing together people with expertise in different academic fields, but the problem must be a narrow one. In other words, technological change is a byproduct of specialization.

Many people attribute economic development to changes in the kind and amount of energy humans use to accomplish their work. In Carlo Cipolla's famous account (1974), the agricultural revolution spurred growth by increasing the efficiency with which humans converted solar energy to food and work. The industrial revolution brought about another leap in efficiency as mechanical energy was harnessed to accomplish tasks, first from renewable sources like falling water or burning wood, and later from fossil fuels. This line of thinking suggests that economic development is ultimately limited by our ability to convert renewable energy to useful work.

It is hard to argue with the fundamental character of energy, or with the empirical correlation of energy use with economic growth. But it is not impossible to conceive of a world in which increased human wellbeing is decoupled from the growth of energy use. If some of us specialize in the problem, we can be smarter about how we use energy. As incomes grow, the mix of goods will shift toward less energy intensity. Then we can have growth without increasing energy use, and a move toward sustainable but expensive energy sources need not burden the economy. The energy intensity of GDP has been falling in the U.S. since the oil shocks of the1970's, and we still have a way to go to match the energy efficiency of other rich countries. The gains-from-trade idea suggests that in principle, economic development does not depend on the growth in the use of any particular good or category of goods, even energy-converting goods.

Explanations of development and growth often focus on the advantages of decentralized market economies and stable legal institutions. That being said, economists have amazingly little faith in the robustness of markets, and so tend to overstate the requirements for markets to function effectively. Specialization and development does not require a complete set of markets, with perfect competition and a uniquely determinate vector of prices. Even bilateral monopoly can give rise to gains from specialization and trade. Market economies are robust, and can survive some social constraints on prices.

Indeed, market-based economic development is entirely consistent with interventions designed to increase income equality. The division of labor is limited by the extent of the market, and a large, thriving middle class is a great way to extend the market. Income inequality introduces social pathologies that are expensive, but necessary, to control (Tiemstra 1992). Productive resources like land are more likely to be effectively employed if they are in the hands of striving workers than in the hands of the very rich.

The benefits of specialization and the gains from trade are sometimes used to justify corporate mergers and other moves toward large size and monopoly power. But the gains-from-trade theorem does not require that specialization take place within a single firm. Quite the contrary—it is an argument for decentralization. As Yang so effectively puts it, "The benefits of the division of labor are network effects rather than effects of the scale of a firm or sector" (2003, p. 68). Trade is generally a good thing, but corporate giantism is not.

THE COSTS OF ECONOMIC GROWTH: THE EARLY LITERATURE

The literature from the 1970's on the costs of economic growth includes highly controversial books from E. J. Mishan (1970, 1977) and Herman Daly (1977), the first report for the Club of Rome (Meadows et. al. 1972), and symposia like the one at Lehigh University in 1972 (Weintraub et. al. 1973). At the same time there were a number of books by Christian commentators (mostly theologians) questioning the affluent lifestyles of western evangelicals, and implicitly criticizing growth. These include prominent works by Ronald J. Sider (1977, 1980), John V. Taylor (1975), and Adam Corson-Finnerty (1977).

These works rely partly on broad empirical generalization and partly on romantic nostalgia. Historically, since the mid-nineteenth century economic growth has been associated with increased use of fossil fuels and degradation of the natural environment. The critics saw the aesthetic costs of pollution diminishing the quality of life even as economic activity grew, and they feared the depletion of natural resources would limit growth.

Today things are both better and worse. Air and water look and smell better than in early industrial times, and economists emphasize that the richer countries regulate pollution, health, and safety more rigorously than poorer countries do. There are better substitutes for fossil energy than there were. But biological diversity seems to be declining everywhere, and the looming effects of global climate change pose a serious threat. For the most part, the environmental question has been separated from the phenomenon of growth. As noted above, I believe that economic growth can be consistent with environmental sustainability, but there is much more to be explored in this question. The character of development has to change, and it won't happen automatically.

The "Little England" nostalgia for an earlier, simpler time infects much of this literature (e.g. Mishan 1977, ch. 28–30; Meadows 1972, pp. 175–78; Sider 1977, ch. 8). The reader pictures tweed-coated academics strolling back from the village to the rose-covered cottage with the makings for dinner and greeting the vicar and Miss Marple on the way. It's rather precious. The reverse side of the tight community and moral consensus of a bygone era was the rigid class structure that precluded a democracy of power and wealth, and stifling conformity and prejudice that punished creativity and ambition. The hardships and lack of opportunity for those at the bottom of the income and social scale are forgotten. I think the criticism was onto something, but because these writers failed to connect social change to the economic development process, they mistook what they were losing.

SPECIALIZATION AND THE COSTS OF GROWTH

If the gains-from-trade theorem shows us the root of economic growth, the logic of the specialization suggests where the costs of growth arise. I wish to discuss three of these: inflexibility of the economy, ecological vulnerability, and shallow social relationships.

Economic Inflexibility

Most of us were trained to think of comparative advantage in a Heckscher-Ohlin world, where the source of the advantage was differences in factor endowments, but resources could always be reallocated among industries costlessly. Changes in the economic environment, e.g. new trade agreements, would lead to changes in the pattern of specialization, but this is achieved instantly and costlessly. In the real world, the comparative advantages of individuals and firms, and hence of countries, arise from education and training, skill and experience, social connections, and highly specialized equipment and buildings. These are difficult, if not impossible, to change in the face of changes in the economic environment. These are the cases where economic change leads to structural unemployment. These transitions are felt the most intensively by workers who are not well educated, and hence have skills which are not easily adaptable to new occupations.

The more highly developed an economy is, the more specialized its workers and firms become, and the more difficult it is to change specialization in the face of new conditions. Also, as an economy grows, its structure tends to change because of changes in demand, as old goods complete their market penetration, and consumer attention turns away from goods to services (Kindleberger 1989). This may be the source of the "economic climacteric" that seems to afflict many highly developed economies, with symptoms of persistent structural unemployment, vulnerability to imports, and lagging productivity growth (Kindleberger 1996).

The coming of the great unspecialized machine, the computer, has softened this problem to some degree, but not entirely. Though engineers have persistently predicted the rise of "flexible manufacturing" made possible by computer-aided design and computer-controlled tools, factories still tend to be quite specialized. This may be partly because businesses searching for market power have an incentive to sink costs in order to create an entry barrier. The more specialized the machine, the more irretrievable the cost.

Vertical integration can also serve quite effectively as an entry barrier, but it also reduces flexibility by reducing the firm's openness to networks outside the organization. Some research suggests that firms in industrial districts, where different process stages are done by different "job shops," are more adaptable than vertically integrated firms (Best 1990; Piore and Sabel 1984). So the private incentive to establish market power by raising entry barriers leads firms both to sink costs and to integrate vertically. But the external consequence of both of these is to make the economy less flexible in the face of change. That change is itself a consequence of growth, because growing affluence changes the composition of the desired consumption bundle.

Ecological Vulnerability

It is a fashion on campuses lately for environmental activists to ask the institution to source food from the local region as much as possible. The rhetoric of this issue relies heavily on emotional appeals, often based in romantic nostalgia for a supposedly simpler time when people were more connected to nature and the seasons. It is counted a virtue to know where ones food originates, and if possible to have a personal relationship with the farmer, if not the cow that provides the milk for ones breakfast cereal. Here in the temperate Midwest a surprising variety of foods can be obtained this way with the right connections and sufficient work.

It is easy to lampoon this effort, but there is a serious argument that could be made for local sourcing of food. It is not the argument that is occasionally made about the environmental cost of transporting food over long distances. At least in principle, it is possible to devise a sustainable system for transporting goods. Indeed, future sustainable economic development and growth depends on our ability to construct such a system. A beginning would be to price fuel so that the environmental costs of transportation are reflected in its money price. We are just at the beginning of serious efforts to implement sustainable transportation, but there are good reasons to expect that this essential task can and will be successfully accomplished.

A more serious objection concerns specialization. The economic development process will lead farmers to specialize in crops for which they have a comparative advantage, and seek to export those crops to the widest possible market. The rationale for specialization and trade in agriculture is the same as in industry: there are efficiency gains to be had from specializing in the area of ones comparative advantage. The result is the modern farm: acres and acres of identical plants, possibly even clones, with no other life as far as the eye can see. Maintaining this ecological anomaly requires huge inputs of petrochemicals, fossil water, and fossil-fuel-driven machinery, but until recently, these inputs have been cheap enough. College dining halls buy from the low-cost provider, as do most purveyors of food.

The difficulty is that these monoculture systems are not sustainable and robust. An infestation of pests, a new disease, or a spell of bad weather can lead to catastrophic failure. Such systems are never observed in nature. They can only be maintained through the use of large inputs of exhaustible resources. In the long run, we will have to find another way to grow our food, fuel, and fiber (Meadows et al. 2004, pp. 57–66). The virtue of local sourcing is that it creates demand for a wide variety of agricultural products in a limited region, which can result in a more diversified, and hence more robust and sustainable, agricultural sector.

This problem can also characterize manufacturing-based economies, and the conurbations that make specialized service economies possible. Any concentrated industry will yield a concentration of waste products, which can easily come to overwhelm the capacity of the natural processes of the local ecosystem to dilute, disperse, or decay. If these are synthetic waste products that do not break down naturally, so much the worse. Those who suffer the most are those without sufficient income to escape to cleaner neighborhoods or regions. The climate-change problem is in a different category, because there it is the global carbon cycle that is overwhelmed by the volume of human emissions.

Clearly, this is one area where negative environmental consequences flow directly from the fundamental mechanism of economic development. To make a diversified, sustainable, and robust ecology we must sacrifice some of the benefits of comparative advantage, specialization, and trade.

Social Superficiality

A lot of the complaints about the social costs of economic growth are sentimental, but there is enough discomfort about the issue to suspect that there is something real behind it. I have come to think that the process of specialization itself works to compromise the depth of human relationships (See also Scitovsky 1964). The effect must be carefully separated from other effects that may be the outcomes of population growth or changing relative prices.

What people miss about the good old times was the depth of relationships that resulted from repeated encounters with the same people in different contexts. In times past, it was very likely that at least some of the people you worked beside were also people you saw at church, in the grocery store and the barbershop, at the children's school and the tavern, and at the lodge or the club. The same lawyer drew up the deed to your house as well as your will, and the same doctor treated your diabetes and attended your children's births. This was as true of urban neighborhoods as it was of small towns and rural villages. It could feel stifling or constricting, especially to young people, but you came to know these people very well, and there is value in that.

As the economy has developed, our relationships have become single-dimensional and superficial. We encounter many people in daily life, and we know very little about any of them, because we only encounter them in a single restricted context. Part of this is simply the outcome of population growth. There are just a whole lot more people around to encounter. Part of it is the change in habits that came with the automobile. Robert Putnam (2000) famously has theorized many causes for a declining level of overall civic engagement.

I think that no small part of it is the outcome of specialization. Since occupations are much more specialized than they were, it is less likely that someone we encounter in our economic role as producer will also show up in some other dimension of life, regardless of how engaged we are in civic activities. It is also less likely that one service provider will be able to meet a wide range of our needs or demands for services, or that the same service provider who meets our specialized requirements will also meet those of our friends. This can be true as much of hairdressers as of doctors.

Leisure activities have also become more specialized in this same development pattern, and so there is a whole crowd of buddies with whom we share a particular recreational enthusiasm, but are unlikely to share anything else. Watching TV can be a solitary experience, and Putnam singles it out as a major cause of social isolation, but it used to provide a common popular culture to many. When there were only three or four channels on the air, TV provided plenty of fodder for water-cooler conversation. It was a true mass medium. The proliferation of cable television channels to suit specialized tastes means it is decreasingly likely that we can even converse with an acquaintance about last night's programs.

THE WAY AHEAD

If specialization and growth are the major causes of these problems, stopping the process is the most satisfying solution. There have been many advocates for regional self-sufficiency and limited growth, especially since globalization has accelerated in recent years. Among the most prominent are Herman Daly (1989), the late E. F. Schumacher (1973), and the late Jane Jacobs (1970). It is easy for affluent Americans to say that we are too preoccupied with growth, too materialistic, and don't pay enough attention to the kinds of happiness that money can't buy. I have preached this often to my students, joining the great chorus of Christian commentators, and the Bible itself: "The love of money is the root of all kinds of evil" (1 Tim 6:10). "But store up for yourselves treasures in heaven" (Matt 6:20).

But surely this neglects the good that comes of economic development. We may not value growth much if it means only that the super-rich add more floor space to their mansions, or that we get another TV so we don't miss a crucial play while in the kitchen fixing a snack. But we became economists because we want to see people prosper. There are many people who need better food, more education, improved medical care, and yes, high-speed Internet access. The value of economic growth depends on the use to which it is put. It is not sufficient for politicians, challenged on "the vision thing," to say that their vision is economic growth. Growth itself is not a moral vision, but only makes moral actions possible. Redefining growth so that we only count "good growth," as in a Tobin-Nordhaus-style "Measure of Economic Welfare" or a Daly-Cobb-type "Index of Sustainable Economic Welfare" does not solve the problem, but only covers it over. GDP is a measure of market activity, not welfare. Devising a new index will not make the need for a measure like GDP go away, and it prejudges the answers to questions about what economic activities really contribute to human well-being and what makes economic growth sustainable.

What then is to be done? The approach of Benjamin Friedman (2005) exemplifies how economists generally deal with these issues. Each of the negative consequences of growth is taken as a separate issue, to be addressed by a benevolent regulator who attacks the problem as close to its root as possible (see esp. chapters 14 and 15), using the appropriate taxes, subsidies, and other policy tools. The main intention is to keep the growth process alive, even as its problems are addressed, but the result is unsatisfying. First, it relies too heavily on government, and too little on business and civil society. We need to involve civil society for its commitment to principles rather than money or votes. To a large and increasing extent, business has bought into the idea of the "triple bottom line," and we need to make use of that. Second, the conventional approach is preoccupied with economic efficiency as the standard for economic performance. Both these issues arise from an over-reliance on the assumptions of standard economic theory: people have no values or goals beyond increasing their own personal economic wellbeing.

In my own work on the flexibility issue (Tiemstra 1994), I have argued that the best solution is not to rely on government-directed industrial policy, but rather to encourage businesses to take the primary role in planning for economic transitions. In the process, managers should value sustainability, social capital and community stability as much as they value market success. Business managers know best what resources they have, and creative, entrepreneurial business leadership should be able to find new and profitable ways to deploy those assets as old industries decline. Finding new ways to make money with old resources is a skill that we value in managers, and that they try to cultivate. Conceived of this way, the process should avoid some of the problems that arise when these decisions neglect the interests of community, or are made exclusively by governments. Whether this type of planning is easier for vertically integrated firms or for firms in industrial districts should be a topic for further research.

Business flexibility should take account of the community's investment in infrastructure. I mean not just the physical infrastructure of transportation, utilities, and basic public services, but also the social infrastructure of civil society. The investments made in social networks by private, voluntary organizations are crucial to the functioning of human community. These investments are discouraged if social networks are constantly disrupted by the changing economic structure of the region. If businesses can respond to new economic conditions without causing such social disruptions, investment in social capital should increase, and the social superficiality that results from economic development can be avoided.

The most daunting, but most necessary, of these transitions is the move to an ecologically sustainable economy. I don't know exactly what such an economy will look like. I can only offer a few thoughts about how to get there. Government policies alone will not be sufficient. Market incentives and business initiatives alone will not be sufficient. The environmental movement alone will not be able to accomplish it. For sustainable growth to occur, it will take the efforts of people of good will in all sectors of society. People must act with the goal of sustainability in view, rather than a narrow focus on economic efficiency.

These efforts need to be coordinated at the local or regional level in order for the pieces to fit together in the end. Since sustainability and community stability are to be served along with economic development, it is unlikely that the coordination task can be accomplished by relying exclusively on markets. There is a role here for regionally based indicative planning. Making sure that investments in community infrastructure are wisely made and effectively utilized requires planning across the boundaries of business, government, and civil society. Since regional ecological diversity is the key to sustainability, regional planning needs to coordinate smaller scale private and public decisions about land use and waste handling. And decentralized businesses can invest and redeploy assets more effectively if the know what other, neighboring businesses are planning. But an essential element of the process is innovation, so any planning process must be open to innovative solutions. Remember, innovation works best when creative people specialize and concentrate on narrowly defined problems. That is the way forward.

It is also the way backward in some ways. Regional, participatory indicative planning is an important feature of the strain of Catholic social thought that is the historical foundation of social economics (McKee 1987, pp. 97–100; Wilber and Jameson 1983, ch. 10). We have a tradition and a literature we can draw on as we put forward the ideas that will make a new, benign form of economic growth possible.

CONCLUSION

Contrary to what many economists seem to believe, economic growth is not the solution to all problems, or the answer to all moral dilemmas. The value of economic growth depends on the uses to which we put it. Growth that only provides more toys for the top third of the population is not worth the costs. Growth that creates better nutrition, health, and education for the bottom half is worthwhile.

Nor is growth the demon that haunts modern society. The fundamental principle of comparative advantage, specialization, and exchange teaches us that growth brings its special problems, which are not automatically solved by decentralized market processes. But these problems are not insoluble. Leadership with a clear vision and firm moral purpose can operate the economy to create new solutions to these problems.

So when our crass, craven politicians suggest that the sum total of their vision for society is more economic growth, we should reject them. When nostalgia-paralyzed romantics want to take us back to life as it was in Native American settlements or English farming villages two centuries ago, we have to say that isn't good enough. With great wisdom and good leadership, it should be possible for us to be both prosperous and happy.

REFERENCES

Best, Michael. 1990. *The New Competition: Institutions of Industrial Restructuring.* Cambridge: Harvard University Press.

Cipolla, Carlo. 1974. *The Economic History of World Population.* Sixth edition. Harmondsworth, UK: Penguin.

Corson-Finnerty, Adam Daniel. 1977. *No More Plastic Jesus: Global Justice and Christian Lifestyle.* New York: Dutton.

Daly, Herman E. 1977. *Steady-State Economics.* San Francisco: W. H. Freeman.

Daly, Herman E., and John B. Cobb, Jr. 1989. *For the Common Good.* Boston: Beacon.

Friedman, Benjamin M. 2005. *The Moral Consequences of Economic Growth.* New York: Alfred A. Knopf.

Gordon, Robert J. 2003. "Exploding Productivity Growth: Context, Causes, and Implications." *Brookings Papers on Economic Activity* 2, 207–98.

Helpman, Elhanan. 2004. *The Mystery of Economic Growth.* Cambridge: Harvard University Press.

Jacobs, Jane. 1970. *The Economy of Cities.* London: Jonathan Cape.

Kindleberger, Charles P. 1989. "Engel's Law" *Economic Laws and Economic History.* The Raffaele Mattioli Lectures for 1980. Cambridge, UK: Cambridge University Press, pp. 3–20.

Kindleberger, Charles P. 1996. *World Economic Primacy: 1550–1990.* New York: Oxford University Press.

McKee, Arnold F. 1987. *Economics and the Christian Mind.* New York: Vantage.

Meadows, Donella H., Dennis L. Meadows, Jorgen Randers, and William W. Behrens. 1972. *The Limits to Growth.* New York: Universe.

Meadows, Donella, Jorgen Randers, and Dennis Meadows. 2004. *Limits to Growth: The Thirty-Year Update.* White River Junction, VT: Chelsea Green.

Mishan, E. J. 1970. *Technology and Growth.* New York: Praeger.

Mishan, E. J. 1977. *The Economic Growth Debate.* London: George Allen and Unwin.

Piore, Michael J., and Charles F. Sabel. 1984. *The Second Industrial Divide: Possibilities for Prosperity.* New York: Basic.

Putnam, Robert D. 2000. *Bowling Alone: The Collapse and Revival of American Community.* New York: Simon & Schuster.

Schumacher, E. F. 1973. *Small is Beautiful.* New York: Harper & Row.

Scitovsky, Tibor, and Anne Scitovsky. 1964. "What Price Economic Growth?" In *Papers on Welfare and Growth,* Stanford University Press. Reprinted in *The Goal of Economic Growth,* rev. ed., ed. Edmund S. Phelps, 31–46. New York: Norton, 1969.

Sider, Ronald J. 1977. *Rich Christians in an Age of Hunger.* Downers Grove, IL: InterVarsity Press.

Sider, Ronald J., ed. 1980. *Living More Simply.* Downers Grove, IL: InterVarsity.

Taylor, John V. 1975. *Enough is Enough.* London: SCM.

Tiemstra, John P. 1992. "Equality and Efficiency: The Big Tradeoff or a Free Lunch?" *Journal of Income Distribution* 2 (2) 164–82.

Tiemstra, John P. 1994. "Competitiveness and Industrial Policy." *International Journal of Social Economics* 21 (8) 30–42.

Weintraub, Andrew, Eli Schwartz, and J. Richard Aronson, eds. 1973. *The Economic Growth Controversy.* White Plains, NY: International Arts & Sciences Press.

Wilber, Charles K., and Kenneth P. Jameson. 1983. *An Inquiry into the Poverty of Economics.* Notre Dame, IN: University of Notre Dame Press.

Yang, Xiaokai 2003. *Economic Development and the Division of Labor.* Malden, MA: Blackwell.

PART 4

Globalization and Competitiveness

13

Competitiveness and Industrial Policy

DEFINING THE PROBLEM

"THE COMPETITIVENESS PROBLEM" MAY not be the most descriptive term to attach to the long-run difficulties the US economy has faced for the last 20 years, but by now everybody knows what is meant by it. The cluster of problems includes a rate of productivity growth that is low by historical standards, a long, slow decline in the average level of real wages, an unsustainably large international trade deficit, and a loss of worldwide market share in key manufacturing industries in which we were once the world leaders. However, once we get beyond that simple description of the problem, there are many differences. The pundits and economists do not agree on the priority of the various aspects of the problem, the underlying causes, the loci of responsibility for dealing with the problems, the policy objectives to be pursued, or the policies that should be adopted.

To professional economists, trained to be concerned about economic growth and the overall standard of living, it is clear that the declining average real wage is the most serious of these problems, and that slow productivity growth is the reason for it. Then the policy objective clearly must be to raise the productivity growth rate, and that means enhancing investment and R&D. The trade deficit did not appear until ten years after "competitiveness" became a concern, and seems to be related more to short-run macro issues. It is important, but it appears not to be responsible for the larger difficulty, and it is much easier to solve. Market shares in manufacturing are of great concern to the business professionals who have contributed to this literature, but to the economists they seem to be a poor proxy for the really important variable, productivity.

What puzzles many economists is that ordinary people are not more upset about declining real wages and living standards. Krugman says, "I find the lack of protest over our basically dreary economic record the most remarkable fact about America today" (1990, p. xi). He puts this down to the diminished expectations of Americans, and expresses his hope that people will be roused to demand that something be done about it (though in the end, Krugman himself does not want to do very much). The election of Bill Clinton can be read as a sign that ordinary people have indeed awakened to Krugman's call.

It is not the decline in real wages that bothers people. They drive an older car than they used to, and they have put off replacing the carpeting and the furniture. They are more concerned than they used to be about losing their health insurance, because it does not take much these days to run up devastating medical bills. They worry about the kids getting out of college with big debts. But life is still pretty good. They still eat well, and go out once in a while. There is a lot of choice on cable TV and the radio, and if all else fails they can rent a video. A vacation is still within reach, though they might not travel as far as they used to. More of this world's goods is not what these people want or need. They want and need some degree of security in their jobs, so that they can fulfil the commitments they have made to their families and communities. And they want and need to get their communities back (Raines et al., 1982).

Ordinary people are upset and have been upset all along. If we consider the popular books and films that have taken this problem as their subject, we find a lot of the protest that Krugman missed. (I am thinking of books like America: What Went Wrong? (Barlett and Steele, 1992) and movies like The Fighting Ministers, Roger and Me, Places in the Heart, Wall Street, and Other People's Money.) The concern is about business and farm bankruptcies and plant closings in the older urban areas of the northeast and the Great Lakes. The problem is that without an economic backbone, people must leave their communities or fall into desperate economic circumstances. Families scatter, community infrastructure is abandoned, institutions wither, and the social fabric disintegrates. It is not the older car or the shorter vacation that bothers people about the competitiveness problem; it is the decline of community.

The cause of these bankruptcies and plant closings has less to do with the rate of productivity growth than it does with changes in the industrial structure of the economy. Slow productivity growth may erode competitive advantage in some industries, but the aggregate figures suggest that most of our most important trading partners also have suffered a productivity slowdown, and our relative position has not changed that much. The competitiveness problem that concerns most people is a problem of transition costs in moving from one industrial structure to another. Unfortunately, transition costs figure in pure economics the way friction figures in pure physics. That is to say, these costs are considered uninteresting and are mostly ignored. I am suggesting that in the last 20 years, these uninteresting and unimportant phenomena have become our country's major economic problem (Magaziner and Reich, 1982, pt III).

In order to consider what policy measures might be appropriate for dealing with this problem, we need to look into the causes of structural change in the US economy, but we also need to investigate the rigidities in the economy that makes this change more difficult, slow, and costly to accomplish. Then we will be able to consider policy approaches.

STRUCTURAL CHANGE IN THE US ECONOMY

There are a number of ways to explain the changing structure of the US economy over the last 20 years. But we should first point out that to some commentators it does not matter what causes the structural changes. Conservative writers tend to claim that structural change, whatever the cause, is inevitable in any economy, and the market process is the best way to handle the transition. It is feared that any government policy intervention will be used only to slow down the transition or to redirect it inefficiently. Hence the wide disdain in this literature for policies that amount to "picking winners and losers" (Davis, 1983; McKenzie, 1988).

The difficulty with this view is its failure to distinguish between statics and dynamics. Economic theory and history teach us that markets lead to a reasonably efficient allocation of resources in an economy that is growing moderately and not changing rapidly in structure. But when growth is sluggish, underemployment of resources is chronic, and economic structure is changing rapidly, it is not at all clear that the unaided market minimizes the costs of transition, provides appropriate incentives to make use of un-employed resources, or distributes transition costs fairly. Economic theory has almost nothing to teach us about this, and the resources of economic history have not been put to work very effectively on the problem. The dis-content with the performance of the US economy over the past 20 years suggests that there is considerable room for improvement.

But it certainly could be the case that the changes in economic struc-ture in the USA have been the result of forces that we might not want to change or be able to change. These might include the change in the rela-tive price of fossil fuels and other natural resources after 1973; the rise of productivity and industrialization in many parts of the Third World; changes in technology that have resulted in reduced communication and transportation costs; and changes in product and production technology as a result of developments in microelectronics. All of these developments are probably beneficial on balance in the long run, and in any case beyond our control (Adams and Klein, 1983).

The large structural fiscal deficits in the USA since 1980 are no doubt responsible for a large part of the unsustainable trade deficits. That is a problem all by itself, and needs to be solved for the economy to be healthy in the long run. But the switch after 1980 to a policy of large deficits coupled with tight money, and then the switch back to easier money and somewhat tighter fiscal policy later in the decade caused changes in the economic structure. The high interest rates and overvalued dollar of the early and middle 1980s caused problems for farming and manufacturing while very much helping the financial services industry. Later changes caused severe problems for financial services while making farming more profitable. Continuing high long-term real interest rates meant that the recovery of manufacturing was never complete even after monetary policy eased and the dollar declined. If unnecessary changes in economic structure are to be avoided, there needs to be a certain consistency to macro-economic policy at the national level, and monetary and fiscal policy need to be better co-ordinated than they have been since the Ac-cord of 1951 (Krugman, 1990, ch. 3).

A number of significant policy changes are in the works presently that could have significant effects on the structure of the US economy. Among them are the downsizing of the military-industrial complex, the North American Free Trade Agreement, the GATT negotiations and the accompanying reforms of agriculture programmes, health-care reform, and the reduction of the federal fiscal deficit. Many of these moves have attracted significant grass-roots political opposition, undoubtedly because the public understands the transition costs involved in them. The Clinton Administration has tried to address these concerns by proposing a national programme for improving the operation of labour markets and the training of displaced workers. Since this programme does not address the question of social and public infrastructure, it is not likely to satisfy the critics. However, this does not mean that the policy initiatives should be abandoned. All of them are aimed at improving the long-run growth and sustainability of the US economy. The President is right to suggest that abandoning them would involve trying to preserve an industrial structure that will not survive market forces much longer anyway.

New developments in international trade and industrial organization (both the reality and the theory) have focused attention on the role of external economies and first-mover advantages in the dynamics of industrial development. In many newer high-technology industries there are significant economies of scale and of agglomeration, learning-curve economies from cumulative production, and differentiated products. The US has failed to grasp (or frittered away) an early lead in some of these industries because of lack of government support, inability to penetrate foreign markets (whether because of foreign market barriers or lack of American interest), or managerial complacency. This failure to compete results in falling market share and output, which makes it necessary to reallocate resources to other industries and incur transition costs in the process. Loss of world market share can occur even if conventionally-measured labour productivity is up to world standards. Once a market lead is gone, the barriers to entry in these industries are nearly insurmountable (Tyson, 1992). In older, low-technology industries it has become ever harder for the USA to compete because of the accelerated speed of technology transfer and the increasing ability of low-wage economies to compete in manufacturing (Reich, 1991). This is the classic meaning of the competitiveness problem, and it is only partly related to the issue of productivity.

It is this argument that provides the best case for industrial policy in the traditional sense, and it is here that the debate becomes the most heated. Are these transitions necessary or avoidable? Should government merely subsidize private R&D through the tax code? Should government hand out money for commercial development projects? Or something in between? Should government merely try to make American markets as open to foreign competition as possible, or try to force open foreign markets, or protect infant industries at home? Should securities and antitrust laws be changed to promote business combinations with deeper pockets and longer time horizons? What should business schools be teaching their students about long-run business strategy? All of these proposals could affect the success of a new industrial structure, but none of them directly address the problem of transition costs.

The changes in the US's industrial structure may only reflect an inevitable ageing of an advanced and growing economy. Engel's Law predicts that as income grows the proportion devoted to food drops, and so a growing economy must undergo structural change as resources are shifted out of agriculture and into manufacturing. Clearly something similar happens at a later stage of development as markets for manufactured goods become saturated and the service sector absorbs an increasing share of the economy's resources. But this latter transition is even more difficult because the capital intensity of manufacturing leads to an accelerator effect. Lower growth rates in consumer goods industries mean a decline in investment and shrinking capital goods industries (Kindleberger, 1989). These changes are inevitable. Trying to slow them down or stop them would be foolish. What is within the reach of policy is to reduce and redistribute the costs of making the transition.

RIGIDITY IN THE ALLOCATION OF RESOURCES

Compounding the problem of structural change in an economy with a slow natural growth rate are various factors that inhibit the movement of resources from one sector or industry to another. These elements of rigidity add to the cost of economic restructuring if we rely on the market mechanism alone. Some of these factors are argued to afflict all ageing industrial economies, and some seem to be unique to the USA.

Olson (1982) has argued that as an industrial economy ages it accumulates a plethora of organized interest groups. These groups acquire power in the marketplace and power in the political system which they are able to use to further their own agendas, mostly involving their members' material wellbeing. The groups with the most advantaged positions are the ones with the most power. This makes the economic structure very rigid, because any pressure for structural change is resisted by these powerful organized interests. This problem becomes worse as the society ages, and can be reversed only by a cataclysmic social upheaval such as a lost foreign war, a civil war or a revolution. The more vigorous societies like Germany and Japan are the ones that have undergone such an upheaval more recently than the declining ones like the USA or Britain. Olson's theory suggests the possibility of a bright future for the eastern European states currently undergoing upheaval.

Klein (1977) carries forward a similar argument. Continuing productivity growth and competitiveness require risk-taking, but the entrenched economic powers in an ageing society, big business and organized labour, are very averse to risk. As these groups are able to make their own situations more predictable, they add rigidity to the structure of prices and the allocation of resources. This makes the economy less stable even as (for many people) it becomes more predictable.

The last few years have seen a decay in the economic power of some of the institutions singled out by Olson (1982) and Klein (1977). Big businesses have lost market share and employment as technology and market conditions have changed and they have been out-manoeuvred by smaller, newer, more nimble firms. Organized labour has lost ground partly because of government policy changes, but also because its fortunes have been tied so closely to big business. However, it has proven more difficult to control the political power of these and other economic interest groups. If we are to improve the ability of the economy to handle structural change with a minimum of cost, it is important that we reform our political process to diminish the power of organized private interest groups.

Some writers have suggested that the difference between competitive and uncompetitive businesses and industries is the ability to respond quickly to shifts in market demand and changes in technology—in other words, flexible production (Piore and Sabel, 1984; Best, 1990). Flexibility involves the way R&D and production are organized, as well as the production technology in use. Though flexible production seems clearly to enhance productivity growth and competitiveness, it is not universally popular. Modern industrial organization theory suggests some reasons (besides sheer habit) why this might be so. One way for firms to deter entry and enhance their own market power is to make a credible threat to engage in predatory pricing. Such a threat is credible if the firm has large sunk costs which would be lost in the event of its exit from the industry. So there is an incentive for firms with high market shares to invest in production technology that is as industry-specific as possible, which is the opposite of flexible production (Stiglitz, 1987). A possible policy approach to this difficulty is to use antitrust enforcement powers to punish predatory pricing when it occurs, and to discourage mergers aimed at vertical integration, which tend to make companies less flexible by discouraging the recombination of different kinds of production facilities.

Modern labour market theory also suggests that there are some reasons that labour has become less flexible as well. The proliferation of knowledge means that workers need to "know more and more about less and less." It may even be true that the knowledge they need is occupation-specific or firm-specific. The market for such workers thus has bilateral monopoly characteristics. In the current policy environment, with its scant support of collective bargaining and the lack of portability of benefits, the business has the larger amount of bargaining power. Firms believe they should be able to treat employment even of highly skilled workers as a variable cost, imposing wage cuts or layoffs in periods of slack demand. This lack of loyalty to the workforce is reciprocated. Workers try to acquire the skills that may be transferable to other lines of work or other firms, but do not work so hard to acquire the more firm-specific skills. Businesses in turn fail to invest in improving the skills of workers who may be laid off or who may leave the firm at the first attractive offer. The result is a labour force with deficient skills and low morale, both of which cause competitiveness and flexibility to suffer (Dertouzos et al., 1989, chs 6,7).

There are a number of policy approaches that could correct some of these problems. Strengthening workers' bargaining power and mobility would decrease insecurity, but at the expense of a co-operative environment in the workplace, and the institutional flexibility that Olson's and Klein's theories suggest is needed. An improved publicly-sponsored training and job-search programme for displaced workers has been proposed by the Clinton Administration. Such programmes have a spotty record, are quite expensive, and involve the government in picking winners and losers among occupational categories and industries. They also fail to address the problem of conserving community assets that is the central concern of most workers. The only complete solution would be for the managers of businesses to increase their loyalty to their labour force by guaranteeing them a degree of income and employment stability, and for workers to reciprocate that loyalty. Only then will both sides have the incentives to invest in productivity-enhancing training and co-operation.

A large part of the resources that must be moved between industries is social infrastructure that is owned in large measure by the government—such things as water and sewerage systems, highways, airports, schools, criminal justice facilities, and the like. The location of this capital literally cannot be changed, so if it is to change sectors, new private investment in new sectors must occur in locations that have been abandoned by declining industries. There is no particular incentive for the private sector to do this since this capital is owned by the government and non-profits. This issue is closely associated in many people's minds with the competitiveness issue, since the interpersonal ties that people value so highly are tied to location in much the same way. Churches, fraternal organizations, affinity groups and family are also part of this immobile social infrastructure (Raines et al., 1982).

Saving the social infrastructure is usually left to state and local governments as a policy matter. This is disastrous because it leads to unseemly and ruinous competitions between local jurisdictions to attract jobs. The passage of "enterprise zone" legislation at the national level is designed to mitigate this problem, but it remains to be seen whether the benefits of this law will be effectively targeted at communities that have suffered serious economic decline and abandonment of the social infrastructure, or whether the benefits will be distributed on the basis of the political clout of areas' lawmakers. Plant closing notification laws are of some help in giving communities and workers a head start on replacing their economic bases.

Nearly every book on the competitiveness problem points to the short time horizons of American managers as a significant cause. What underlies this attitude is harder to tell. Some writers believe it is simply the low net national savings rate and the resulting high cost of capital in the USA that explains the problem. There are some difficulties with this explanation, but it has some merit. Other commentators believe that the structure of capital markets in the USA and the effect of this structure on corporate governance is the root cause. Very few stockholders in this country have long-term commitments to the businesses they partly own. This is even true of the institutions, like pension and mutual funds, that now own the bulk of outstanding equities, and who follow the "Wall Street role" of selling rather than reforming poorly performing businesses. As a result there is too much focus on short-term financial performance, and changes of control are too easy to accomplish. These features are reflected in the incentive structure of executive compensation (Dertouzos et al., 1989, ch. 4; Jacobs, 1991).

Policy approaches can range widely. Some argue that reducing the federal budget deficit would increase net national saving and reduce the cost of capital, with significant beneficial effects. Raising private saving through changes in the tax code, particularly a move towards consumption taxes, has been suggested, but seems unlikely to be very effective. Taxing transactions in the stock market has been offered as a way of encouraging long-term investment, but this too seems likely to be ineffective. Anti-takeover legislation could address the problem, but leads to prolonged and expensive litigation, and could have the drawback of entrenching ineffective management. Reforms in banking regulation could lead to more patient ownership of industrial firms by banks, as is the case in Germany and Japan, but open up the danger of more concentration of economic power than Americans are comfortable with.

But the problem may not be simply the result of external forces. Many writers have suggested that short planning horizons (and some of these other problems) may be the product of American management culture. American schools, with their long-standing assimilationist mission, have traditionally de-emphasized foreign languages and cultures, and so American managers have tended to ignore or dismiss foreign markets and competition. The superpower status of the USA may also have contributed to a certain arrogance among American managers. Since the 1960s business school education has been based more thoroughly on economic theory, which has led to an emphasis on short-term financial management, has stressed the adversarial character of labour-management relations, and has de-emphasized the importance of specialized industry knowledge, instead suggesting that managerial skills are easily transferred between industries. Marketing and finance have been the fashionable specialities, while manufacturing and operations management have suffered a lack of prestige. As the problems of structural change have been ignored within mainstream economic theory, they have not been addressed in the business school curriculum (Dertouzos et al., 1989, chs 3, 4).

These are not the kinds of issues that can be addressed by government economic policy. They involve changing attitudes, values, behaviours and policies in a wide variety of social settings and institutions, most of them within the private sector. Fortunately a large part of the competitiveness literature is addressed to readers in the business community, and so it leaves behind the economists' assumption that all firms behave alike, and focuses instead on professional management practice. While much of the advice that is offered is valuable, it sometimes reinforces the idea that there is a general formula for good management that works no matter which company or industry it is applied to, and thus underplays the importance of industry-specific knowledge.

Finally, there is mounting evidence that a large part of the competitiveness problem is a result of underlying social problems. The education received by the bottom half of the labour force, the people who do not attend college, is not adequate for the demands of modern industry. The schools bear some responsibility for this, but a large proportion of these students come from poor or lower class homes, and that contributes to the problem. The enormously high crime rates in this country add to the tax burden for supporting a large criminal justice system, and impose security costs and direct losses on businesses. Environmental problems are made worse by poverty, and businesses are asked to pick up the cost. The problems of the cost and coverage of the medical care system need only be mentioned here (Bailey et al., 1993; Bluestone and Harrison, 1988; Litan et al., 1988; Thurow, 1985).

The connection between social problems and the competitiveness issue is underappreciated by all sectors of American society. People perceive the solution of social problems as a costly luxury that we can afford to address only when our economic problems are under control, not as an investment in the solution of our economic problems. They also perceive social problems to be almost completely intractable. These perceptions are probably wrong. There are many promising approaches to solving our social problems that we have not yet tried on a national scale. Until these unhealthy perceptions change we will not be able to muster the political will to tackle our economic or our social problems.

THE GOALS OF COMPETITIVENESS POLICY

It is futile to try to use industrial policy to prevent structural change. If such change could be prevented it would solve the problem, but market forces in an integrated world are too powerful to resist. A country that tries to use trade barriers or subsidies to keep obsolete industries alive is only incurring greater costs and exacerbating the competitiveness problem. The great fear of the opponents of a classical industrial policy of subsidies to particular industries is that political pressures will push those subsidies towards the industries of the past rather than the industries of the future. This fear is undoubtedly justified, and we should not rely too heavily on an industrial policy that tries to pick winners and losers or that tries to preserve the present industrial structure of the economy forever. Policies should be pursued which remove roadblocks to constructive industrial change, like NAFTA, GATT, and military downsizing. The structural changes these policies represent offer long-term gains if the transitions can be managed appropriately. Furthermore, those structural changes may be unavoidable anyway. The only caveat is that there should be consistency and co-ordination of monetary and fiscal policy so that unnecessary and spurious changes in industrial structure are avoided.

If competitiveness policy is to be a constructive and dynamic force, indeed if it is to work, it must recognize the inevitability of a certain amount of structural change. Policy then must aim at accelerating the process of industrial change, reducing its cost and redistributing its burden so that it does not disproportionately affect a few people and communities. The policies discussed in the preceding section are aimed at reducing the barriers to structural change, reducing its cost and accelerating the process.

There are also some policies that can help to redistribute the burden. A properly targeted national programme of "enterprise zones" or "empowerment zones" could offer financial inducements for businesses to locate in areas where abandonment of social infrastructure has occurred or is threatened. Thus it could not only reduce the waste of social infrastructure and give businesses incentives to make use of idle resources; it can also shift the cost of dealing with the problem to the national taxpayer base and away from the already strapped local community. Done properly it should also preclude destructive competition for industrial development between various state and local governments. It is unfortunate that Washington gridlock has prevented an effective programme of this type from being implemented.

Whether a similar kind of programme to relieve the burden on displaced workers and save wasted labour resources can be effective is more problematical. Trade adjustment assistance tried to be such a programme, and was widely judged to be a failure. Workers tended not to use the assistance for retraining and moving, preferring to use it to tide them over until the old jobs came back. This is a powerful testimony to the power of community in people's lives, and a hint that this sort of programme needs to be coupled to an "enterprise zone" programme in order to work. Government-run training programmes have some of the aspects of picking winners and losers, since some particular occupational skills have to be offered, and government has an indifferent record predicting which occupations will grow the fastest. It makes more sense for government to encourage businesses to retrain their employees. This could be done by offering tax credits for training, or by penalizing businesses that fire redundant employees rather than retraining them.

MAKING THE TRANSITION

Conventional economic theory leads us to ask whether structural changes in the economy should be brought about by market forces, shrinking and bankrupting old firms and bringing new entry in new industries; or by government planning, with committees or bureaucrats moving resources by directive from sunset industries to sunrise industries, from losers to winners. The market solution is efficient and dynamic, but leaves behind destroyed communities and redundant workers. The government solution is more equitable, but would probably be inefficient and, in the end, futile. Given such a choice, most thoughtful people choose the market.

But there is another choice that incorporates the benefits of plan and market. Let the transition from one economic structure to another be planned, but not by some government committee or agency, but by the managers of the companies involved. As managers of private-sector companies, these executives would have every incentive to pursue activities that could be expected to be economically viable in the future, and would have a better sense of what those activities might be than would the local government officials who are often left by default with the job of finding new businesses to make use of existing local resources. In entering new product lines private managers would be following the direction of the market. But the resources of the firm—whether people, buildings or equipment—would not have to become unemployed and seek out alternative work in a market where information and incentives are incomplete and distorted. The accumulated organizational experience of the firm, such as its network of contacts and its habits of working together, would not be dissipated. And the collectively-owned community infrastructure, about which people care so deeply, would not be wasted. The firm would incur some transition costs, but the total social transition costs would be much reduced.

This is not the kind of strategy that is often pursued by big businesses and conglomerates. These firms often diversify or move from one industry into another, but they do it by buying and selling existing businesses, or by shutting down old plants and opening new and totally unrelated ones. Often they "diversify" by pursuing vertical integration, which makes it harder for them to make a transition from one industry to another later on. Some pursue the General Motors' strategy of closing old plants and opening brand new, greenfield plants in distant locations to do essentially the same work. These strategies are easy ways for management to enhance its own job security, but they do not make good use of the firm's or society's existing resources. In Japan, the large industrial groups have often shifted employees from one company to another related one, enabling the larger corporations to offer guaranteed lifetime employment. This system seems to be breaking down during the current recession, with many workers sitting in offices but having nothing to do. This phenomenon underlines the difficulty that very large corporations have in managing these transitions, even in an institutional environment that encourages it. Moving people around the company is not the answer. New activities must be found for old work groups to perform.

A strategy of managing transition within the firm is also not a likely choice for very small businesses, if only because they have limited financial resources for sustaining a transition and severely limited access to managerial expertise that might be required for such a transition. The most likely firms to pursue internally managed transition are medium-sized manufacturing firms, probably with a single plant though not necessarily with a single line of business, or similarly sized units of larger businesses that have a high degree of managerial autonomy. Antitrust policy could probably be used to encourage the existence of firms of this size.

Would such an approach represent "profit-maximizing" behaviour by the firm? Certainly the kinds of choices we are discussing are not marginal adjustments in the quantity of production or the input mix, but rather discrete choices of strategic direction. A high level of uncertainty is involved—financial results could be extremely profitable or disastrous. The transition costs that would be minimized are largely external to the firm, which is why such business decisions are today often left to governments, who are not equipped to make them well. The only possible conclusion is that the neoclassical concepts of the profit-maximizing firm and the externality-managing government are not useful in addressing this problem.

However, we can say that this approach to the competitiveness problem does require a change in American management culture. It requires managers to think strategically and to adopt a long-term horizon. It requires them to know their companies very well and to have a deep understanding of the demands not only of their own business, but of related businesses as well. But most of all it requires a change of attitude. Managers must think not only of their own job security or "maximizing shareholder wealth" when making strategic decisions. They must identify with the firm they manage instead of identifying with some elite, footloose, abstract managerial profession. They must think of themselves as stewards of all of the resources, human and non-human, tangible and intangible, that the company has put together over its history. They must take responsibility for finding useful employment for those resources by exploring every opportunity in the marketplace and pursuing every linkage with other businesses that might bring in profitable work. The incentives for managers to do this would not primarily be pecuniary ones. Managers would achieve job security for themselves, and the loyalty of the workforce in their company would likely result in increased productivity. But the main external reward to managers for this kind of behaviour would be the esteem of the community.

It is not government policy but business policy that will solve the competitiveness problem of the USA. We are a country well endowed with experienced, educated business managers. When we begin to make full use of that resource, we will be well on our way to competitiveness again.

REFERENCES

Adams, F. G., and Klein, L. R. (1983), "Economic Evaluation of Industrial Policies for Growth and Competitiveness: Overview," in Adams, F.G. and Klein, L.R. (Eds), *Industrial Policies for Growth and Competitiveness*, Lexington Books, Lexington, MA.

Bailey, M. N., Burtless, G., and Litan R. E. (1993), *Growth with Equity*, Brookings, Washington, DC.

Barlett, D. L., and Steele, J.B. (1992), *America: What Went Wrong?*, Andrews and McMeel, Kansas, KS.

Best, M. (1990), *The New Competition*, Harvard, Cambridge, MA.

Bluestone, B., and Harrison, B. (1988), *The Great U-Turn*, Basic, New York, NY.

Davis, J. M. (1983), Making America Work Again, Crown, New York, NY.

Dertouzos, M. L., Lester, R. K., Solow, R. M., and the MIT Commission on Industrial Productivity (1989), *Made in America*, MIT, Cambridge, MA.

Jacobs, M. (1991), *Short-term America*, Harvard Business School, Boston, MA.

Kindleberger, C. P. (1989), Economic Laws and Economic History, Cambridge University Press, Cambridge.

Klein, B. (1977), *Dynamic Economics*, Harvard, Cambridge, MA.

Krugman, P. (1990), *The Age of Diminished Expectations*, MIT, Cambridge, MA.

Litan, R., Lawrence, R. and Schultze, C. (Eds) (1988), *American Living Standards: Threats and Challenges*, Brookings, Washington, DC.

PART 4: Globalization and Competitiveness

Magaziner, I., and Reich, R. B. (1982), *Minding America's Business*, Vintage, New York, NY.

McKenzie, R. (1988), *The Great American Jobs Machine*, Cato, Washington, DC.

Olson, M. (1982), *The Rise and Decline of Nations*, Yale, New Haven, CT.

Piore, M. J. and Sabel, C.F. (1984), *The Second Industrial Divide*, Basic, New York, NY.

Raines, J. C., Benson, L. and Gracie, D. (Eds) (1982), *Community and Capital in Conflict*, Temple University Press, Philadelphia, PA.

Reich, R. B. (1991), *The Work of Nations*, Knopf, New York, NY.

Stiglitz, J. E. (1987), "Technological Change, Sunk Costs, and Competition," *Brookings Papers on Economic Activity*, Vol. 3, pp. 883–947.

Thurow, L. C. (1985), *The Zero-Sum Solution*, Simon & Schuster, New York, NY.

Tyson, L. D. (1992), *Who's Bashing Whom? Trade Conflict in High-technology Industries*, Institute for International Economics, Washington, DC.

14

Financial Globalization
and Crony Capitalism

INTRODUCTION

MANY ECONOMIC TRANSACTIONS ARE characterized by asymmetric information; that is, one of the parties is more aware of or has more control over the circumstances and performance of the transaction than the other party has. This is particularly true when money is lent. The borrower typically has a better idea of and more control over what the money will be used for, and the risks involved in that use, than the lender does. Any transaction that involves the extension of credit or the expectation of future performance by one party may have similar characteristics. Asymmetric information can inhibit transactions if lenders believe that borrowers will typically behave in opportunistic fashion and exploit their informational advantage. At worst, the financial system could be dysfunctional and economic development could be retarded.

This problem is handled in different ways in different cultures. A traditional, closed society with a high degree of cultural homogeneity might develop a widely shared sense of solidarity and "fair play" that would inhibit opportunistic behavior. A more pluralistic society might develop a system where networks of people who are related by ethnicity, family, religion, class, school ties, or some other bond would deal preferentially within the network, excluding those outside the network. We might call this "crony capitalism." Large, modern pluralistic societies might develop elaborate means for reducing the incentives for opportunism, requiring borrowers to make large down payments, put up collateral or performance bonds, hold compensating deposits, and so on. Such contracts can become very complicated, and elaborate legal process is usually available to enforce their terms. We could call this the "litigious society."

Which of these approaches a society adopts will depend a great deal on its size and degree of heterogeneity in culture, religion, and race. It will also depend on the widely shared ideological and religious values within that society.

CRONY CAPITALISM

Opportunistically taking advantage of people, especially in a business relationship, is something that usually will work only once. "Fool me once, shame on you; fool me twice, shame on me." Having an ongoing relationship between business partners is a deterrent to the abuse of asymmetric information, because sacrificing the relationship forecloses too many future opportunities for profitable deals. When a relationship is multi-dimensional, there are many avenues open for retaliation against a business partner who behaves badly. This is the most obvious when family relationships are involved. Families have non-economic ways of punishing opportunistic behavior. Favoring family means you tend to be dealing with people whose character you understand, whom you will deal with repeatedly in economic and non-economic contexts, and who have a moral loyalty to you because of the family connection. So in the family context, opportunism is less likely than it would be with strangers. The elaborate means we in the West use to thwart opportunism are less necessary where the loyalty of family can be assumed. However, a family orientation may inhibit the formation and institutionalization of large-scale industrial enterprises, as Fukuyama suggests (1995, ch. 7). But even when large corporations are involved, the Asian practice of preferential dealing within "families" of companies affords this kind of protection. The traditional practice of "relationship banking" in the Western world indicates that the advantages of "crony" relationships are not lost on lenders in the West, either.

The "crony capitalism" approach to asymmetric information is consistent with, and reinforced by, some aspects of Asian and Islamic cultures. Of course, all of these cultures have traditions that call for hospitality toward strangers and guests, but there is a firm line drawn between insiders and outsiders.

In the Islamic world, outsiders were traditionally labeled "infidels"; to the Chinese they were "barbarians." Bernard Lewis's book (2002) about the encounters between the Islamic world and the West make it clear that there was enough hostility and suspicion on both sides to make the relationship difficult from the start, but it is tempting to conclude that "What went wrong" in the Islamic world was the failure to embrace the non-discriminatory principle that Westerners value so highly. Many Western observers tend to think that the economic development of those countries is inhibited by the tendency not to deal with outsiders. Other analysts would point to the history of Western hostility towards Islam as providing plenty of justification for Muslims to by wary in dealing with the West.

Chinese economic culture represents another example. The Chinese are famous for favoring those with family connections in their economic dealings. Many observers have credited this aspect of their culture for the great commercial success of Chinese communities around the world (Lodge 1995, Fukuyama 1995, chs. 8 and 9). This "family values" approach to commerce has also led to tremendous resentment of the expatriate Chinese, because of the way it closes off economic opportunity to non-Chinese, even natives in their own country. This approach may play a role in both the recent success of the economy of China, as well as the difficulty in incorporating China into the WTO. National treatment of exporters of financial services has been particularly difficult to achieve with China (and other Asian economies), perhaps because this is exactly where asymmetric information is most problematical, and therefore favoritism is likely to play the largest role.

Most of the literature about the relationship of crony capitalism to the Asian financial crisis is not about this kind of asymmetric information issue. Rather, it suggests that the problem was straightforward corruption. Government officials were willing to use public funds to guarantee bank loans to private borrowers with family or political connections to the government (Krugman 1999, pp. 88–9). In this form of moral hazard, taxpayer funds were misappropriated by unaccountable politicians. In the financial collapse and subsequent macroeconomic crisis caused by the overvaluation of many of the Asian currencies, many of these loans went bad. Drawing on the economics of loan guarantees, some of the literature suggests that this increased the vulnerability of the Asian economies to financial crisis (e.g., Heslag and Pecchenino 2005). Krugman is more inclined to think that it merely touched off a garden-variety bank run, and he points out differences between more developed economies, particularly South Korea, and some of the others (1999, pp. 98–101). If government corruption is really the issue, banking system reforms will not solve the problem. Rather, the corruption problem needs to be addressed at its root.

THE LITIGIOUS SOCIETY

Economic culture and economic science in the West have stressed treating each transaction as a separate, independent event, for which the best deal must be negotiated. The competitive forces that guarantee marginal cost prices and efficiency in the allocation of resources can only work if every transaction must be won by hard competition. Furthermore, if there is to be equal opportunity for all comers, including small, unknown businesses, new start-ups, and people from traditionally excluded groups; then cronyism is out. Crony capitalism and ongoing relationships are frowned on, so other methods must be found to deal with imperfect information. Arm's-length negotiations are normative. The exceptions we observe only prove the rule.

Then how does Western capitalism deal with the problem of asymmetric information? Transactions have to be structured in such a way that there are incentives for the parties not to act opportunistically. These include provisions like large down payments, collateral, disclosure of financial statements and credit ratings, insurance, restrictive financial conditions, call provisions, and the like. The transaction has to be formalized in a way that is enforceable at law. Contracts are complicated and long, they have to be written by legal specialists, and very often they must be litigated. As we have learned to our sorrow, this is very costly.

At the source of the principle of non-discrimination is the Judeo-Christian moral tradition. Hans Küng points out that one of the principles basic to most religions and moral systems is the Golden Rule: Do unto others as you would have them do unto you (1998, p. 98). He proposes this principle as the foundation for a global economic ethic. A familiar, nearly equivalent formulation is: Love your neighbor as you love yourself. But the ancient question comes: who is my neighbor? The rules and regulations of the Hebrew Bible call for hospitality to be shown toward foreigners, but there are some distinctions made in the treatment of Israelites and others. For example, the usury regulation prohibited charging interest on loans to Israelites, but not to foreigners.

While the New Testament still teaches that there are special charitable obligations toward those of the "household of faith," most moral distinctions between insiders and outsiders are erased. Jesus answers the "Who is my neighbor?" question with the story of the Good Samaritan (Luke 10: 25–37), and Paul says there is neither Jew nor Greek in Christ (Colossians 3:11).

Still, the usury rule was a troublesome issue for the Christian church down to the time of the Reformation in the sixteenth century. Then the reformer John Calvin made the case that the rule should no longer apply among Christians. The argument had two prongs. Calvin read the usury rule of the Hebrew Bible as meaning to protect the poor, and therefore it should not apply to loans made for commercial purposes. But he also made an argument that built on a kind of universalism in the New Testament. Calvin noted that the usury rule made a distinction between Israelites and foreigners, and therefore must be something less than an absolute moral standard, since such standards must apply to everyone. Since Christians did not recognize any moral distinction between insiders and outsiders, only the universal moral law should apply to Christians' dealings with everyone. Therefore charging interest on loans was morally acceptable, even among Christians (Nelson 1949).

This is how Calvin earned his propers as the founder of Western-style capitalism. It is not so much that he opened the way for a market in fixed-interest loans. Modern Muslims have demonstrated that you can run a modern market economy without interest-bearing financial instruments (though some financial devices they use can resemble fixed interest very closely). The more important contribution he made is the argument that in economic life, everyone should be treated equally. When it comes to economic transactions, there is no ethical reason for treating people differently based on family, religious, national, or ethnic connections. Calvin's main principle was that economic transactions should offer substantial benefits not only to both parties involved, but also to the community at large (Calvin 1999, p. 222). Intellectuals in the Western tradition came to think of the idea of non-discrimination as the foundation of economic theory and a source of the efficiency of market economies. Extended to political, civil, and even intellectual life, it also becomes a basic principle of Western democracy, and the American ideology of equal opportunity.

Not that the West has completely stifled its discriminatory impulses over the last 500 years. Protectionist impulses in the U.S. still seem more likely to be directed most vigorously against those most different from us— those of different civilizations (in Samuel Huntington's (1996) scheme), like the Mexicans or the Japanese. Indeed, support for NAFTA seemed as much based on hope for reducing Mexican immigration to the U.S. as on hope for U.S. economic gains. But the principle of non-discrimination is still there, and it establishes the presumption that we will favor free trade and national treatment unless it is not reciprocated.

Litigious societies are also subject to corruption. The collapse of Enron and other recent scandals have exposed lending practices in the banking industry based on maximizing fee income for bankers and deceptively pumping up securities prices to enrich executives, rather than being based on sound banking principles. These practices not been sufficiently common to result in major bank failures or systemic problems, but consensus partially attributes the 1990's stock-market bubble and 2000–01 collapse, and the resulting recession, to corruption in corporate America, including major money-center banks. Only adroit action by the Federal Reserve prevented a full-blown crisis.

THE RULES OF GLOBALIZATION

Economic globalization now extends to a global market for financial instruments and services. Banks and brokerage houses are now global businesses, bringing together borrowers and lenders across national, cultural, and religious boundaries. Under these new circumstances, how should we handle the problem of asymmetric information?

There are three possibilities. One is to impose one model, the litigious society model, on the whole world. This appears to be the direction in which the world is being led by the International Monetary Fund and the other global organizations that the United States dominates. This approach addresses the asymmetric-information problem, it elevates the non-discrimination idea to a universal principle, and it makes the global system consistent by extending to finance an analog of the "national treatment" principle that has been so effective in promoting free trade in goods.

However, it means serious, disruptive cultural change in societies outside the West. Even here in the U.S., we have begun to question the high costs that extensive litigation imposes on us.

But this approach is not necessary. Another possibility is to allow different countries to maintain their different systems, and require each financial institution to pick a home country whose rules will govern its approach to lending. Financial companies could still operate around the globe, but foreigners then would be aware of what rules would govern their relationships with each institution, and could choose based on their own cultural preferences or financial advantage.

The third possibility is to give up financial globalization as a goal and an ideal. There are some economists and commentators who believe that this sacrifices too much of the gains in development and efficiency that come with globalization. Some would even say that it is inconsistent with globalization in goods markets. But others have argued that globalization of financial markets is not an inevitable consequence of globalization in goods markets, and that globalized financial markets pose too many risks for financial crises, like the Asian crisis of the mid-1990's (e.g. Bhagwati 2000).

A PLURALISTIC APPROACH

Hans Küng to the contrary notwithstanding, the moral quality of non-discrimination is not universally appealing. Even in the West, while we deplore racism, sexism, and chauvinism, we still admire genuine patriotism, family values, and loyalty to church and community. In economic life, even after the last twenty years of celebrating our flexible labor, financial, and other markets, we still find to it be useful, if not admirable, to have some degree of loyalty between employer and employee, and between vendor and customer. The model of human behavior governed almost exclusively by economic incentives is not very appealing, because it seems to suggest that people should behave opportunistically when they can get away with it (behavior that the Christian Reformers would have strongly condemned). This model also misleads us when it suggests that economic transactions always can be made "incentive-compatible," so that there are no incentives to cheat or behave opportunistically, making trust unnecessary. The "moral capital" of trust is necessary for a market economy to function efficiently, as Fred Hirsch pointed out long ago (1976), and has been reiterated by Fukuyama (1995).

The rules of the global economy rightly suggest that when national governments decide to open their borders to trade and investment, national treatment (i.e., imports treated the same as goods of domestic origin) is the appropriate policy. But this does not say anything about the behavior of private economic agents. Private economic favoritism may be frustrating to foreigners, and it may have an illegitimate racial dimension. But eliminating favoritism of all kinds is not necessary to the proper functioning of a market economy in the global context. Indeed, for the global market economy to function properly, people have to be able to choose to deal with those whom they can trust. In the West we have elaborate rules excluding discriminatory criteria. But when it comes to international law, instituting rules to eliminate favoritism and crony capitalism unnecessarily invites conflict between countries with different religious and cultural foundations.

It is hard for us as Westerners to give up the principle of non-discrimination. We should continue to hold it as an ideal in our own societies. The principle of the moral equality of all humans is one of the glorious and unique characteristics of Western civilization. It is also a necessary thing in our own societies. Our U.S. society is deliberately a pluralistic one, where immigrants of different races and creeds can come and continue to develop their own cultures, while contributing to the common culture. We Americans have also taught ourselves that in economic life, it is acceptable, even good, to look out for our own individual interests and not worry about the interests of others. We have adapted our institutions to make this principle work reasonably well in our economy, but it doesn't always fit other societies. We must be wary about imposing this idea on others, and we must be very careful about assuming that people of other cultures and religions will accept the superiority of non-discrimination and will practice it rigorously.

REFERENCES

Bhagwati, Jagdish, 2000, *The Wind of the Hundred Days*, Cambridge: MIT Press.

Calvin, John, 1999, "Letter on Usury," in Denis R. Janz, ed., *A Reformation Reader*, Minneapolis: Fortress, pp. 219–22.

Fukuyama, Francis, 1995, *Trust: The Social Virtues and the Creation of Prosperity*, New York: Free Press.

Heslag, Joseph H., and Rowena Pecchenino, 2005, "Crony Capitalism and Financial System Stability," *Economic Inquiry* 43(1), January, pp. 24–38.

Hirsch, Fred, 1976, *The Social Limits to Growth*, Cambridge: Harvard University Press.

Huntington, Samuel P., 1996, *The Clash of Civilizations and the Remaking of World Order*, New York: Touchstone.

Krugman, Paul, 1999, *The Return of Depression Economics*, New York: Norton.

Küng, Hans, 1998, *A Global Ethic for Global Politics and Economics*, New York: Oxford University Press.

Lewis, Bernard, 2002, *What Went Wrong? Western Impact and Middle Eastern Response*, New York: Oxford University Press.

Lodge, George, 1995, "The Asian Systems," in Stackhouse, et. al., 1995, pp. 754–57.

Nelson, Benjamin N., 1949, *The Idea of Usury: From Tribal Brotherhood to Universal Otherhood*, Princeton, NJ: Princeton University Press. Excerpted in Stackhouse, et al., 1995, pp. 265–71.

Stackhouse, Max L., Dennis P. McCann, and Shirley J. Roels, eds., 1995, *On Moral Business: Classical and Contemporary Resources for Ethics in Economic Life*, Grand Rapids: Eerdmans.

15

The Social Economics of Globalization

THE GLOBALIZATION OF THE economy has been a prominent topic of public debate at least since the 1999 Seattle meeting of the World Trade Organization filled the streets with protest demonstrations by environmental, labor, consumer, religious, and other civil society groups. But the roots of that debate were formed in the competitiveness controversy of the 1980's and 1990's, and the policy path that it questions goes back to decisions made beginning in 1944 at the Breton Woods conference. The economic crisis of the 1970's accelerated globalization by giving new impetus to neo-liberal economic ideology, embodied by the rise to power of Ronald Reagan and Margaret Thatcher. Technological developments that reduced the costs of transportation and communication accelerated the trend.

How are we to understand the current state of this debate? In the social economics tradition, we look first at the moral values that are at stake. These values are important not just for normative insight into economic policies, but also for the light they shed on the behavior of different parties in the economy, and the arguments of different advocates in the debate.

As is true of most arguments over economics, the values that we want the economy and economic policy to serve are mostly beyond dispute. It is hard to challenge the desirability of prosperity, sustainability, and cultural diversity. Disagreements over values tend to focus on peripheral issues. Rather, the major argument arises over the predictions of economic theories (Tiemstra 1998). Will continued economic globalization promote these widely held values, or undermine them? To understand the debate, we must examine and assess the theoretical claims of the different sides.

Because we begin with the premise that ethics matter in economics, our criteria for the assessment of these theories will include their openness to the possibility of moral choice. Though economics is often described as "the science of choice," it too often accepts a mechanical, deterministic view of economic processes that in effect denies the possibility of choice (Lawson 1997, chs. 13, 19). If economic motivation is accounted for exclusively by material self-interest, and economic power is constrained by pervasive competitive forces, there is only one way things can turn out. Such an account denies freedom of choice and moral responsibility, turning people into "globules of desire" and the economy into a giant computer.

A useful theory of globalization would account for how globalization changes the opportunities for different actors, recalibrating the balance of power in society. The point of this is not to calculate a new equilibrium, but to understand how to bring different actors together to accomplish the goals that we all seek.

THE MORAL GOALS OF GLOBALIZATION

Prosperity

The main point of economic globalization is to promote economic growth by increasing the extent of the market, and thereby deepening the division of labor and specialization. This economic growth is a precondition for reducing the incidence of poverty worldwide, and enhancing the standard of living and life chances for everyone.

Globalization is justifiable only if it results in the reduction of poverty without compromising the wellbeing of ordinary folk. It is not justifiable if the benefits of growth accrue predominantly to the affluent. We regularly see cases in the U.S. where workers are told that their pay is being cut or their jobs eliminated because of globalization, which will ultimately lead to economic growth. But growth for whom? Why should people of modest means make sacrifices to increase the wellbeing of those who are already better off? For that matter, why should the poor of one country be asked to sacrifice for the benefit of the poor of another country? The only acceptable answer is that the growth resulting from globalization must benefit all (DeMartino 2000, ch. 3).

The absolute level of real incomes is not the only issue here. If poverty is defined to exist when income inequality grows too large, then that has to be considered too. Globalization that makes incomes more unequal within national or regional societies fosters injustice, exploitation, lack of access to social institutions, and diminished social solidarity. This is true even when everyone's real incomes have increased by the usual measures. In a world of instant communication and a homogenized popular culture, inequality can also become a problem when international gaps become too large. International resentment is the result, and global good will is too fragile to take much of that either. The importance of inequality is the main contested value in this area.

This is a demanding standard. Economic growth is one thing, but a distributional norm is a high threshold, even if it is confined to increasing absolute incomes. Yet we will see that the proponents of globalization do not back away from claiming that globalization benefits everyone, a theoretical claim that critics vigorously contest.

Sustainability

In economics we are used to thinking of sustainability as simply a question of whether the economy is investing enough in tangible and intangible capital that the level (or rate of growth) of consumption can be sustained. Our growing understanding of the interaction of ecology and economy has led us economists to include ecological capital in this equation. Economic development and growth in the past have been associated with serious environmental deterioration. Environmental deterioration can cause aesthetic problems that compromise the quality of life, especially for the poor. More seriously, many major threats to human health have environmental causes, and the loss of ecosystem diversity can add to those problems as well as frustrate the search for solutions. Economic productivity can be reduced by the depletion of environmental resources. This raises questions about whether globalization-induced growth is self-limiting or ultimately impossible.

Globalization proponents understand the value of the environment as arising from the use that humans make of it, so they are not surprised that environmental damage is more tolerated in countries with lower income levels. This is consistent with their prediction that rising income levels will lead to more demand for environmental protection.

Dialogue with thinkers in other fields like biology, earth science, and ethics teaches us that more is at stake. The conditions that allow the earth to function as an ecosystem are threatened by human activity. The integrity of the ecosystem depends on the quantity and quality of economic activity. Ecological sustainability has become an economic issue. The critics of globalization see the value of the environment as transcending human use and subjective desire. They are therefore not content with instrumental approaches to the sustainability issue, such as those that rely on cost-benefit analysis, or rely on economic demand as a measure of ecological value. This complicates the policy-making process by insisting that policy-makers make ethical value judgments, rather than relying on calculations or measurements by expert social scientists to settle contentious policy issues.

Cultural Diversity

Cultural change is inevitable as international communication, travel, and trade expand. But as much as we lament the decline of traditional crafts, games, stories and music (in our own country as much as elsewhere), it is not just the influence of Hollywood movies and Nashville music that raises these concerns.

Part of culture is the ways in which we carry out business transactions. What are the rights of buyers and sellers, or employers and employees? What rights come with patents and copyrights? What can be done with a handshake, and what needs to be written down? How do we handle asymmetric information and conflict of interest? What do we do about market power? Different cultures make different choices about how to handle these issues. These choices are based in the most profound beliefs about basic ethical principles and the nature and purpose of human life, and they usually have religious roots. Diversity in these cultural practices is valuable, and should be maintained. (Tiemstra 2006; Pot 2003; Stiglitz 2006, ch.4).

There is a tendency in the secularized West to believe that there is one set of "best practices" that answers all these questions in a way that maximizes efficiency and growth. In the name of economic rationality, everyone ought to accept and adopt these best practices. But what if these practices are incompatible with a culture or religion? Can a nation choose to maintain its traditional economic practices, and still enjoy the benefits of globalization? Can a country be modern, i.e. economically developed, and not be culturally Western? Can we have our Lexus and our olive tree, to use

Friedman's famous metaphor? While pro-globalization secularists demand conformity to Western practices, Islamic fundamentalists see those practices as opposed to true piety. Some theologically conservative Christians also have doubts about the impersonal economic rationality that globalization seems to demand (Goudzwaard 2001). The questions remain open.

MAINSTREAM THEORIES OF ECONOMIC GLOBALIZATION

Advocates of Globalization: Neoliberalism and Market Competition

The core supporters of globalization adopt a rather rigid form of neoclassical economics that has come to be called "neoliberalism." This analysis proceeds from the assumption that globalization has pushed both product and factor markets further than ever in the direction of perfect competition. It is more sophisticated than the traditional Heckscher-Ohlin-Samuelson model, however, because it does not hold technology and relative factor supplies constant, but rather tries to account for how they change over time.

Thus, while the H-O-S theory predicts that the relatively scarce factor in each country will see its real price fall when trade is opened up (the Samuelson-Stolper Theorem), the neoliberal school predicts that returns for all factors will rise in all countries as globalization proceeds. This results from "ladders of comparative advantage." Low-income countries begin by specializing in unskilled-labor intensive goods, but as they develop, capital grows faster than the labor force, and sophisticated technology is imported or developed. The growth of goods markets worldwide leads to more intensive specialization, which increases total factor productivity in poor and rich countries. Comparative advantage then shifts emerging market countries to the export of more sophisticated goods. Factor market competition makes real wages rise in both the importing and exporting countries. Everybody benefits (Bhagwati 2004, pp. 123–7).

Changes to comparative advantage are costly, because they imply shifting resources among industries. The incidence of these costs sometimes falls on those who already have relatively low incomes, particularly unskilled workers in developed countries like the U.S. The most thorough of the globalization advocates propose that these low-income people who suffer from globalization should be compensated by some special form of assistance, along the lines of the Trade Adjustment Assistance program that was long a part of the U.S. system. The gains from globalization should be sufficient to fund such a program many times over. However, these economists believe that most of the decline in incomes for unskilled workers in the U.S. have resulted from the nature of technological change over the last three decades or so, and not globalization.

When it comes to pure inequality, there is a genuine difference concerning the normative goal. Most globalization advocates do not believe that increased inequality is a problem as long as the status of the least-well-off is improved (Bhagwati 2004, pp. 66–7). They hold this to be true internationally as well as within countries. To express it somewhat differently, they hold an absolute definition of poverty rather than a relative one. This is consistent with the usual textbook version of utility theory that economists teach, though it is not consistent with modern psychological research, or with economic research on the effect of inequality on the well-being of low-income people (Frank 1999, ch. 5).

Globalization advocates treat the environment as a production input that also gives utility to its owners, much like a worker's time. As productivity and incomes grow, more environmental resources will be used for production at first. But continued income growth will lead people to withdraw these resources from the market in order to consume them directly. The story is very much like the backward-bending labor supply curve, but it is expressed as an "environmental Kuznets Curve," with environmental quality first decreasing and then increasing as per-capita incomes grow (Bommer 1998, ch. 2). Genuinely global environmental problems like ocean pollution and climate change can be handled by international agreements (Bhagwati 2004, ch. 11). Sophisticated multinational companies will use state-of-the-art, clean technology because it saves costs (Porter and van der Linde 1995), or because it is needed to make products acceptable in developed country markets (Vogel 1995, ch. 8).

This analysis is based on the economic assumptions that a rich, unused environment is a legitimate part of a country's comparative advantage, and that there are always substitutes for the environment in production and consumption. There is also a normative assumption that the environment does not have any moral value apart from human use. The natural ecosystem is assumed to have only instrumental value, and sustainability is viewed in strictly economic, not ecological, terms.

Though many globalization advocates believe firmly in the value of cultural diversity, they see it as being enhanced by a global market for cultural products and by pressure from business and the developed world to adopt U.S.-style political institutions. Everybody has their own story to tell, and they can all compete on equal footing in the world cultural bazaar. The growing taste for novelty and adventure in the West obviates any supposed advantage for Western cultural products. However, business practices, legal institutions, and economic policies are seen as purely instrumental, not cultural. (Friedman 2000, ch. 3).

Critics of Globalization: Country Competition and the "Race to the Bottom"

The critics of globalization also embrace the idea that the global economy has intensified competition, but the competition is between different countries for job-creating investment. In the U.S. we have long seen a process that pits different states against each other in a competition for investment that leads to "corporate welfare" and "competition in laxity." According to the critics, the growth of direct foreign investment and "outsourcing," vanishing barriers to trade, and the deregulation of global financial markets, have made this competition spread to the world as a whole, with disastrous results.

Critics claim that just as with states and cities within the U.S., countries adopt the idea that reduced unit labor costs will attract investment and employment. To keep those costs down, they are tempted to relax wage and hour regulation, regulation of workplace health and safety standards, and codes that enable workers to organize and bargain collectively. Businesses often are encouraged to locate their operations in free trade zones, where subsidized infrastructure is made available, where workers are separated from their families and communities, and civil society organizations, journalists, and law enforcement can be kept away. International agreements and organizations can extract promises that standards will be enforced, but there is no mechanism for accountability, and large incentives to cheat. Stories of outrageous working conditions are common (Greider 1997, ch. 15; A. Goldsmith 1996). The possibility of outsourcing or relocation to low-wage countries provides leverage for companies to extract concessions from workers in the developed countries, leading to an increase in wage inequality and poverty in the U.S., Canada, Europe, and other developed lands (Betcherman 1996; Schmitt 2000; Wilterdink 2000).

Critics point out that businesses promising large investments can demand various subsidized inputs from developing countries. Perhaps more important, they can get favorable tax treatment, which starves the public sector of revenue. Unlike the large developed countries that can run deficits with impunity, the IMF and World Bank demand balanced budgets, forcing reduced spending on social services and regulatory enforcement (Epstein 1996; Stiglitz 2006, ch. 2). The result is reduced standards of living for workers, and environmental deterioration.

Globalization critics also see a race to the bottom in environmental regulation. Any costly or burdensome regulation can deter investment, and so there is pressure to reduce these standards or keep them low. Developing countries may lack a sophisticated understanding of the environmental consequences of new business activities with which they have no previous experience. Multinational businesses will bring the most polluting parts of their production processes to the poorer countries to take advantage of the poor countries' tolerance of highly polluting production. Sheer increases in manufacturing and transport activity will also contribute to increased pollution and resource depletion (E. Goldsmith 1996).

These problems can be particularly dangerous in the critics' view, because they understand the environment to be intimately connected to human health and the very survival of the planet. They do not believe that there are always substitutes for the services of the environmental ecosystem, which they believe also has moral value in its own right.

Similarly, they believe that cultural diversity has value in its own right, and may contribute to the survival of the human species. The power of the multinational corporations and the developed-country governments they influence to dictate business practices, legal institutions, and economic policies worldwide denies the value of self-determination, democratic governance, and religious and cultural liberty and diversity (Kalb and van der Land 2000; Kloos 2000). Countries like the United States pave the way for their home-based corporations' success by insisting on uniform institutions and business practices throughout the world. This includes intellectual property rules, accounting and reporting standards, banking practices, tax policies, and the like. While it is reasonable to expect that traded goods should meet the health and safety standards of the importing country, there is no particular reason that business practices and economic policies should not reflect cultural diversity. A diversity of approaches to economic issues might provide some interesting natural experiments in economics.

Competing Theories of Global Competition: A Critique

The proponents and critics of globalization do have relatively minor differences in their understanding of the normative issues that are at stake. While both sides hold that globalization should make everyone better off, the critics argue that economic inequality is a problem in its own right, and proponents tend to dismiss it as normatively unimportant. Both sides would like to see the quality of the natural environment improve, but the critics believe that natural ecosystems have value independent of human use, while proponents think of them as having only instrumental value. Both sides seek to preserve cultural diversity, but the proponents have an instrumental view of business practices and institutions, while critics attribute value to the cultural diversity embedded in these institutions. On the whole, I believe that the critics have the better of it on the normative issues.

The major disagreements have to do with economic analysis, and predictions of the consequences of an increasingly globalized economy. Neoliberals claim that everyone will benefit from globalization, except perhaps for a few victims of the transition who are not compensated. The critics claim that globalization depresses wages and working conditions for many people worldwide, especially unskilled workers, and increases inequality both between countries and within them. Neoliberals predict that environmental quality will improve with globalization-generated development and growth, while critics believe it will deteriorate. Proponents see globalization enhancing cultural diversity, self-determination, and democracy, while critics see these values as endangered.

The theories propounded by both of these groups share common assumptions, and they share some of the same problems. Both sides believe that globalization increases the pressure of competition on businesses, individuals, and governments. In this intensified competitive environment, any entity that does not pay attention to maximizing its own economic status will be literally unable to survive. A business that does not maximize profits will lose its customers and starve for capital, ending in liquidation or merger. A country that does not match competitive moves to attract investment will find itself with a failing economy and a bankrupt public sector. An individual who does not take the multinational corporation's last best offer will be unemployed and homeless. Whichever view you take, globalization can have only one outcome.

Both theories therefore share the awkward determinism that so often plagues the science of choice. Whatever good intentions people may have, whatever their cultural preferences, their moral and religious beliefs, or their personal tastes, their behavior must be driven by self-interested gain-seeking. The impersonal force of competitive markets guarantees that only one outcome is possible, and any effort to change this outcome will result in worse problems than were supposed to be solved. The neoliberals believe the outcome will be benign. The critics believe that the only way to promote moral outcomes is to stop globalization by protecting domestic goods and labor markets and regulating international capital movements.

By denying that economic agents, especially multinational corporations, have the freedom and the power to choose, both theories fail to account for important observed phenomena. For example, the neoliberals have difficulty explaining how growing income inequality and falling real wages for the unskilled in the developed countries can be fully accounted for by technological change, unless we simply assume that technology is the "god of the gaps" that accounts for all otherwise unexplained phenomena. Nor does it make sense of threats regularly issued to U.S. workers to move their jobs to Mexico, China, or some other low-wage country if they do not accept pay cuts. It also fails to account for the decline in the well-being of many farmers and workers in the developing world.

On the other hand, the critics have trouble explaining how the state of California can maintain higher environmental and safety standards for automobiles and other products in the face of competition from other states, let alone other countries. Their theories fail to explain the continued success of the Scandinavian welfare states, and the rise of large middle classes in China and India.

POWER IN BUSINESS

An adequate theory of globalization must account for the shifts in power among the business sector, the government, and the moral-cultural sector, consisting of universities, publishers and journalists, churches, and other public-interest organizations (Novak 1982, ch. 9). It must analyze the possibilities for reestablishing a proper balance in those powers, so that each sector can effectively hold the others accountable. Such a theory should point to policies that can be undertaken in all sectors in order to realize the moral goals for globalization that we all agree are important.

The major effect of globalization on the economy is to increase the power of the business sector at the expense of governments and moral-cultural institutions. It is this disruption of the power balance that gives rise to most of the concerns about globalization. The sources of this shift are the increased mobility of transnational corporations, a reduction in product market discipline, and an increase in capital market discipline.

Mobility

The reductions in barriers to trade and direct foreign investment, and the reductions in communication and transportation costs, enable businesses to move their operations and enter markets virtually anywhere they want to. This mobility gives businesses the alternatives that enable them to exercise strategic bargaining power over workers, governments, and moral-cultural institutions.

The most obvious use of this power is in the threats that corporations make toward their workers to close plants and move jobs if pay, benefits, working conditions, and job security are not sacrificed. In the global economy, workers are still relatively immobile, restricted not only by immigration regulations, but also by language, culture, and family ties. This gives employers the upper hand.

Business mobility is also an issue in bargaining between businesses and governments. Governments generally wish to attract direct foreign investment and market entry by multinational enterprises. This is a source of employment and economic development for the people of the country. Even where the government is corrupt and insensitive to its people, new businesses can still be a source of revenue for the government itself. The issues involved include labor regulation, environmental, health and safety regulation, taxation, subsidies of various kinds, and other favors. Businesses can gain the upper hand by threatening to move. They can also influence governments by making campaign contributions to politicians, and by providing information and helping to frame the terms of policy debates.

Mobility also gives business advantages over moral-cultural institutions. Most of these groups are geographically limited in their scope, and many of them face tight budget constraints. Multinational enterprises can evade accountability by moving sensitive activities away from areas where they are easily accessible to activists, journalists, or scholars. Businesses and wealthy individuals have become more deliberate about making charitable donations to groups that reflect their point of view. They are also more purposeful about exercising control over the editorial positions of the media outlets they own.

Product-market Discipline

Intensified product-market competition is a key part of the neoliberal case that the advantages of globalization are passed on to consumers broadly. Barriers to international trade can also serve as barriers to entry by foreign firms into domestic product markets. Certainly we can all testify that many markets for manufactured consumer goods offer more choice, higher quality, and lower prices than they did in the days of cozy domestic oligopolies. This is especially true in larger and richer countries. But that should not blind us to the fact that new entry barriers have arisen in place of the old ones. These too enhance business power and discretion.

Even with greater numbers of competitors in rich country markets, product differentiation still offers a substantial pricing power advantage to recognized brands. Consumers are still loyal to their favorites, even if there are nine rivals in the market instead of three. Product differentiation also serves as an entry barrier in its own right.

In the global economy there are fewer safe incubators where infant businesses can get a protected start. High trade barriers meant that many countries had their own home grown, small manufacturing industries. Many times these companies remained small, inefficient, and subsidized. But sometimes, when they were well managed and innovative, they broke out of their domestic markets to challenge established multinational enterprises. It is harder to start small in a global market where you compete with the largest firms from the very first (Hymer 1976, pp. 85–96). These days many of these "national champion" small manufacturers are being absorbed by global corporations.

The success of many global firms in exercising monopsony power over their suppliers has convinced many firms to engineer global-scale mergers and alliances in the pursuit of pecuniary economies of scale. Coupled with the use of new supply-chain management techniques made possible by networked computers, this type of market power drives the success of global retailers like Wal-Mart. Manufacturers too are following this path. Not only does this prompt moves to accumulate countervailing upstream market power, it also creates a cost penalty for newer, smaller businesses attempting downstream entry. Such alliances also allow businesses to share information about their costs, and make sure that costs are more uniform across competitors. This makes tacit collusion on pricing decisions easier, even if the alliances do not create opportunities for explicit collusion.

Globalization has created "winner take all" markets in many businesses where competition once may have been the norm. The ease and low cost of international communication has meant that production cloning, network economies, and other self-reinforcing processes work world-wide, and this gives large amounts of market power to the people or corporations at the top of their industries. This not only accentuates inequality in incomes, but also may lead those below the top to lose in absolute terms (Frank and Cook 1995).

Capital-market Discipline

There are a number of ways that corporations could use the market power they have. In the days of protected markets and "big three" oligopolies, corporate leaders often used their market power to provide high incomes and job security to their rank-and-file workers, to fund civic projects, to create architectural monuments and natural reserves, and for other high-minded purposes. It may have been paternalistic, and priorities may sometimes have been misplaced, but businesses had a loyalty to and concern for the communities in which they operated, which led to many worthwhile projects. Globalization has undermined this sense of corporate social responsibility in a number of ways.

The pervasive use of corporate mobility as a bargaining tool in negotiations with workers and vendors has undermined the sense of commitment to community that was once a common part of corporate culture. If you are going to threaten to move to increase your bottom line, then you have to be willing to follow through on that threat. Any program that betrays a sense of commitment to community has to be abandoned in order to maintain a credible bargaining position. Any charitable project has to be cloaked in an ostensible business purpose to avoid the appearance of loyalty. When charitable institutions seek corporate support, they no longer get questions about how the grant will serve the public purpose, but rather how the grant will enhance the donor's public image. There are no more public affairs departments in corporations, only public relations departments.

But perhaps the most damage has been caused by the globalization of capital markets, the group that Thomas Friedman (2000) so colorfully dubbed "the electronic herd." Investors can now search the whole world for profitable opportunities, and so more and more the people with money to invest are relying on professional money managers, mutual funds, hedge funds, insurance companies, pension funds, and other market intermediaries. These intermediaries are judged by a uniform, easily measured criterion: how much money do they make? In turn, they demand that the companies in which they hold large equity positions use their market power to create the highest possible returns for investors, and no other purpose.

The removal of regulatory barriers to international capital movements has been accompanied by the spread of information. It is easier now for money managers to investigate investment opportunities around the world. The growth of business journalism has meant that it is also easier for investors to assess the performance of their favorite investment or intermediary. The new bandwidth has not been devoted to making the information richer or subtler, but rather to instantaneous updates of a few selected market prices and other indexes of performance.

The electronic herd has adopted the neoliberal ideology as their own. Many of them hold it for serious reasons, but they are encouraged to do so by conservative opinion leaders in government and the moral-cultural sector (especially economists). Neoliberal rationalizations enable them to argue that their preoccupation with profitability ultimately benefits everyone. So they continue to pressure corporations to put profits ahead of any other purpose. In the absence of such pressure, corporations would find it less necessary to resist demands for socially responsible activities and behaviors. Local media and local investors would have a greater understanding of such issues than the international business media and money-center financial analysts.

POWER IN GOVERNMENT AND MORAL-CULTURAL INSTITUTIONS

Government

Government is disadvantaged relative to business because governments are not mobile like businesses are in a global economy. Governments are defined territorially, and so are restricted in the face of business threats to move. Whether a government is interested in the welfare of its people or not, it still has a motivation to attract investment, and so has to provide an attractive environment for international investment, unless it wants to be isolated and poor like North Korea.

Furthermore, governments find themselves at the mercy of the electronic herd in much the same way non-financial businesses do. Governments that do not meet the financial market's standards for sound monetary policy, a favorable tax climate, and fiscal rectitude find themselves disadvantaged in the competition for funds. Governments can turn to the IMF or the World Bank, but often they find that the conditions imposed by these official lenders are every bit as stringent as those required by the electronic herd (Stiglitz 2006, ch. 8). This is a significant constraint on government power.

Still, there are some considerations that give governments some power and discretion if policy-makers learn to use them effectively. Governments of countries with large or rich markets can be advantageous locations for businesses that need to be close to their customers. This includes many manufacturers and service companies whose products must be tailored to specific customer requirements that vary by country. Countries with important natural resources hold special interest for certain kinds of businesses (Jenkins et al. 2002). An abundance of educated and skilled labor can attract business to a country, as Ireland and India have learned. All of these advantages can give governments some bargaining power.

Governments also have the advantage of being able to collude openly with other governments to enhance their power over business. For this to happen, there has to be some degree of international consensus that every country could benefit by restricting business, and agreement on the particular standards that should be required. Many of the most successful international agreements are in the area of the environment, health, and safety. While media coverage tends to focus on areas of disagreement (particularly climate change), there are many successful programs on such topics as sanitary standards for food, ozone-depleting chemicals, trade in endangered species, and others (Young et. al. 1996). It is harder to achieve agreement in areas related to labor regulations because of the wide variation in living standards. But even then, there are agreements on such issues as child labor and prison labor. Globalization critics sometimes embrace the argument for collusion, since it suggests a way around the forces of inter-governmental competition.

Government leaders also have a lot of power to lead through the use of rhetoric. Politicians in democratic societies, and to a degree even in non-democratic ones, have to keep in touch with the people. They need to be able to articulate their programs and goals in terms of widely held social values. By shaping this kind of discussion, they can provide both business and the general public with a vision of the direction society should take. Business leaders take this seriously. Businesses in the U.S. today are acting on their understanding of the way the future will be, as political leaders describe it: a pension system with less reliance on Social Security, a health care system in which competition (managed or not) will be used to control costs, an energy system much more dependent on biofuels and hydrogen, and so on. Political leaders have a strong influence on business through this channel.

Moral-cultural Institutions

As discussed above, many activist civil-society organizations, like ecological, peace, and social justice groups, have limited budgets and geographic scope. This limits their ability to serve as a countervailing power to the business sector. Businesses frequently can hide their activities from inquiring private groups. It also is possible for businesses to pit different groups, sometimes in different countries, against each other. Business leaders use their control over philanthropy to control the moral-cultural sector agenda (Hertz 2001, ch. 8).

But the moral-cultural sector includes many types of organization, some of which have global reach. Universities tend to be bound by place, but international networks of scholars can pursue important issues of global scope. Some of the larger news organizations also have capabilities to gather information on a global scale. Declining communication and transportation costs make this kind of global reach more affordable for a greater range of organizations. This enables them to draw attention to the issues of globalization, and to hold business accountable for the use of its power.

Global cooperation or "collusion" is also more possible for mission-driven or issue-driven civil-society groups. These include churches, labor unions, environmental organizations, professional societies, civil rights activists and universities. It is becoming more common for these groups to hold international conventions to focus particularly on the problems of globalization. These meetings enable groups in different countries to reach a common understanding of the normative goals of globalization, a common analysis of its effects, and a common message to present to governments and businesses around the world. It also enables them to share information about how globalization is working on the ground, and to hold the other sectors accountable for their contributions to the problems that exist. Again, globalization critics sometimes embrace this as a way to frustrate forces of international competition.

This increased capability for international cooperation has been accompanied by an increased interest in and openness to input from civil society on the part of intergovernmental organizations. Virtually all meetings of IGOs now make explicit provision for parallel meetings of NGOs, and for discussions to take place between the two sectors. Thanks to the controversies over globalization, and the very visible protests mounted at some of these meetings, they also attract more attention from the media than has been common in the past. This also increases the power and influence of the moral-cultural sector (Bhagwati 2004, ch. 4; Sandbrook 2003, pt. 4).

POSSIBILITIES FOR RESPONSIBLE GLOBAL CAPITALISM

Limiting the Globalization of Financial Capital Markets

Fundamentally economists believe that economic development and growth are the products of comparative advantage, specialization, and exchange. Furthermore, "the division of labor is limited by the extent of the market," as we all learned early on. Therefore, progress in raising the living standards of the poor requires that international trade in goods and services be liberalized.

The liberalization of international movements of financial capital is a different story. Many economists who are strong supporters of free trade in goods nevertheless have strong reservations about free trade in securities. For the most part, these objections are based on the fundamental instability of financial markets, and the lack of institutions that are fully capable of dealing with international financial crises (Bhagwati 2004, ch. 13; Stiglitz 2006, ch. 9). The global financial crisis of 1997–8 was a wake-up call for many people about the dangers of globalized financial markets.

The analysis presented here suggests that there are additional reasons for limiting the globalization of financial markets. First, it is the pressure of the electronic herd for steadily increasing quarterly profits and stock prices, and steadily falling taxes and transfer payments, that results in many of the problems of globalization. Corporations that might otherwise include workers and communities in the prosperity of the business find themselves under perpetual pressure to use their power for the exclusive benefit of their stockholders and top executives. Governments that aim for widespread prosperity find themselves pressured to provide "corporate welfare," austerity budgets and lax environmental and health regulation instead.

Beyond the issues of prosperity and sustainability, the electronic herd also compromise diversity. By insisting on the seamless integration of financial markets worldwide, the advocates of globalization devalue the differing traditions and cultural values that underlie differing practices concerning financial reporting and the treatment of asymmetric information issues. Globally integrated financial markets also make it impossible for different countries to pursue independent monetary policies that suit their circumstances and values. Cultural diversity, democracy and self-determination are sacrificed to satisfy the preferences of the powerful.

Restraining financial globalization requires concerted international governmental action. These actions could take a number of forms. The most popular proposal in the literature is a tax on international currency transactions (a "Tobin tax"). This would discourage short-term, speculative movements of financial capital (Kennedy 2003). There could also be restrictions on the ability of investors to repatriate their profits within a certain time frame, or restrictions on the amounts and kinds of securities that foreigners could hold. Designing restrictions of this type is the kind of exercise many economists enjoy greatly, but it is beyond the scope of this paper.

International Agreements on Labor, the Environment, and Diversity

As noted above, there are already a number of successful international agreements on the environment. Governments and environmental organizations need to continue working to use this device to improve environmental conditions worldwide. There are cases, especially in developing countries, where helping the very poor avoid destitution can have beneficial environmental effects. This is not because they demand aesthetic amenities, as the neoliberal view would have it, but because they would no longer have to resort to desperate but ecologically catastrophic activities like slash-and-burn farming or living in garbage dumps (World Bank 1992).

A major complaint of the globalization critics has been that environmental considerations have been ignored in trade agreements and enforcement actions that arise from them. Fortunately, in recent years public pressure from environmental NGOs has begun to change in this situation. Countries in the WTO are being given more discretion to regulate products for environmental, health, and safety reasons, and labeling has emerged as a way to give consumers more choice over how they deal with the environmental issues connected with consumption (Bhagwati 2004, pp. 150–61).

The issue of the distribution of the benefits of globalization is much more difficult to deal with. Labor standards vary widely among countries based on degree of development and for various cultural reasons. Some important critics have pointed out that trade agreements themselves are often structured to give most of the benefits of trade to the developed countries by preserving subsidies and protection for farming and manufacturing in the developed world. The Doha "development round" of trade negotiations collapsed in failure when the U.S. and the E.U. proved unwilling to drop these protections. A real development round of trade negotiations would help this problem (Stiglitz 2006, ch.3). Politically, such an initiative may have to wait until there is clearer evidence that globalization has broadly benefited the population of the developed countries.

There is no doubt that unskilled jobs will continue to move toward those parts of the world where unskilled labor is abundant. But many businesses cannot move away from the developed countries, and they have the market power to keep prices and wages at remunerative levels. The stagnation of wages in the developed countries like the U.S. may be partly a product of technological change, but it also has to do with a change in social mores that overestimates the contribution of top management and investors, and undervalues the contribution of the work force to business success. Governments can use minimum wage regulation, wage subsidies, transfer payments, regulations favoring collective bargaining, and other devices to address this problem (Mishra 1999, ch. 7; Bardhan et. al. 2006).

Cultural diversity is already an issue in trade negotiations when it comes to cultural products like magazines, books, and movies. Cultural diversity in business practices has attracted less attention, certainly in the U.S. De-globalization of financial markets will help this problem. This is an issue that educational institutions need to address. The economics profession needs to revive the study of comparative economic systems, to focus on how business practices and economic policies vary among market economies, and how economic issues can be addressed in different ways.

Moral suasion

It is important for leaders of all three sectors of society to keep their focus on the three major normative objectives that globalization is supposed to serve. Business, government, and moral-cultural leaders have to use economic analysis to relate their proposals and decisions back to the impact they can be expected to have on prosperity, sustainability, and diversity. It is important not to confuse the theories with the goals, which is why the goals always have to be reiterated by leaders from all sectors of society on all sides of the issue.

These goals and values are nearly universally accepted, but it is easy to lose focus on them if the leaders and their vocal supporters are themselves benefiting from the policy. Under these circumstances, it can be tempting to blur the distinction between norms and theories, to borrow some of the consensus about norms for the contested theoretical claims. Leaders must be held to account by the media and by public intellectuals for their analytical arguments, especially if the evidence does not support the contention that their policies are serving the commonly accepted goals.

REFERENCES

Bardhan, Pranab, Samuel Bowles, and Michael Wallerstein, eds. (2006). *Globalization and Egalitarian Redistribution*. Princeton: Princeton University Press.

Betcherman, Gordon. (1996). "Globalization, Labor Markets, and Public Policy." In Boyer, Robert, and Daniel Drache, eds. *States Against Markets*. London: Routledge, pp. 250–69.

Bhagwati, Jagdish. (2004). *In Defense of Globalization*. New York: Oxford.

Bommer, Rolf. (1998). *Economic Integration and the Environment*. Cheltenham, UK: Edward Elgar.

DeMartino, George F. (2000). *Global Economy, Global Justice*. London: Routledge.

Epstein, Gerald. (1996). "International Capital Mobility and the Scope for National Economic Management." In Boyer, Robert, and Daniel Drache, eds. *States Against Markets*. London: Routledge, pp. 211–24.

Friedman, Thomas L. (2000). *The Lexus and the Olive Tree*. New York: Anchor.

Frank, Robert H. (1999). *Luxury Fever*. Princeton: Princeton University Press.

Frank, Robert H. and Philip J. Cook. (1995) *The Winner-Take-All Society*. New York: Free Press.

Goldsmith, Alexander. (1996). "Seeds of Exploitation: Free Trade Zones in the Global Economy." In Mander, Jerry and Edward Goldsmith, eds. *The Case Against the Global Economy*. San Francisco: Sierra Club, pp. 267–72.

Goldsmith, Edward. (1996). "Global Trade and the Environment." In Mander, Jerry and Edward Goldsmith, eds. *The Case Against the Global Economy*. San Francisco: Sierra Club, pp. 78–91.

Goudzwaard, Bob. (2001). *Globalization and the Kingdom of God*. Grand Rapids: Baker.

Greider, William. (1997). *One World, Ready or Not*. New York: Touchstone.

Hertz, Noreena. (2001). *The Silent Takeover: Global Capitalism and the Death of Democracy*. New York: Free Press.

Hymer, Stephen H. (1976). *The International Operations of National Firms*. Cambridge: MIT Press.

Jenkens, Rhys, Jonathan Barton, Anthony Bartzokas, Jan Hesselberg, and Hege Merete Knutsen. (2002). *Environmental Regulation in the New Global Economy*. Cheltenham, UK: Edward Elgar.

Kalb, Don, and Marco van der Land. (2000). "Beyond the Mosaic." In Kalb, Don, Marco van der Land, Richard Staring, Bart van Steenbergen, and Nico Wilterdink, eds. *The Ends of Globalization*. Lanham, MD: Rowman and Littlefield, pp. 273–80.

Kennedy, Joy. (2003). "Currency Transaction Tax." In Sandbrook, Richard, ed. *Civilizing Globalization*. Albany: SUNY Press, pp. 111–19.

Kloos, Peter. (2000). "The Dialectics of Globalization and Localization." In Kalb, Don, Marco van der Land, Richard Staring, Bart van Steenbergen, and Nico Wilterdink, eds. *The Ends of Globalization*. Lanham, MD: Rowman and Littlefield, pp. 281–98.

Lawson, Tony. (1997). *Economics and Reality*. London: Routledge.

Mishra, Ramesh. (1999). *Globalization and the Welfare State*. Cheltenham, UK: Edward Elgar.

Novak, Michael. (1982). *The Spirit of Democratic Capitalism*. New York: Simon and Schuster.

Porter, Michael and Claas van der Linde (1995). "Toward a New Conception of the Environment-Competitiveness Relationship." *Journal of Economic Perspectives*. 9(4) Fall, pp. 97–118.

Pot, Ferrie. (2003). "Globalization of the Employment Relationship." In Dolfsma, Wilfred, and Charlie Dannreuther, eds. *Globalization, Social Capital and Inequality*. Cheltenham, UK: Edward Elgar, pp. 118–43.

Sandbrook, Richard. (2003). *Civilizing Globalization: A Survival Guide*. Albany: SUNY Press.

Schmitt, John. (2000). "Inequality and Globalization: Some Evidence from the United States." in Kalb, Don, Marco van der Land, Richard Staring, Bart van Steenbergen, and Nico Wilterdink, eds. *The Ends of Globalization*. Lanham, MD: Rowman and Littlefield, pp. 157–68.

Stiglitz, Joseph E. (2006). *Making Globalization Work*. New York: Norton.

Tiemstra, John P. (1998). "Why Economists Disagree." *Challenge: The Magazine of Economic Affairs*. 41(3) May-June. pp. 46–62.

Tiemstra, John P. (2006). "Financial Globalization and Crony Capitalism." *Cross Currents* 56(1) Spring, pp. 26–33.

Vogel, David. (1995). *Trading Up*. Cambridge, MA: Harvard University Press.

Wilterdink, Nico. (2000). "The Internationalization of Capital and Trends in Income Inequality in Western Societies." In Kalb, Don, Marco van der Land, Richard Staring, Bart van Steenbergen, and Nico Wilterdink, eds. *The Ends of Globalization*. Lanham, MD: Rowman and Littlefield, pp. 151–56.

Young, Oran A., George J. Damko, and Kilaparti Ramakrishna, eds. (1996). *Global Environmental Change and International Governance*. Hanover, NH: University Press of New England.

World Bank. (1992). *Development and the Environment.* New York: Oxford University Press.

www.ingramcontent.com/pod-product-compliance
Lightning Source LLC
Chambersburg PA
CBHW061220220326
41599CB00025B/4698